It Will Never Happen to Me

It Will Never Happen to Me

Growing Up with Addiction as Youngsters, Adolescents, Adults

Claudia Black, Ph.D.

Second Edition

Hazelden
Center City, Minnesota 55012-0176

1-800-328-0094
1-651-213-4590 (Fax)
www.hazelden.org

©1981, 2001 by Claudia Black
All rights reserved.
First edition published by ACT, 1982
Second edition published by MAC Publishing, 2001
First published by Hazelden, 2002
Printed in the United States of America
No portion of this publication may be reproduced in any manner without the written permission of the publisher.

ISBN: 1-56838-798-9

06 05 04 6 5 4 3

Interior design by Rachel Holscher
Typesetting by Stanton Publication Services, Inc.

Except for the poetry and the story "Best Little Boy in the World," names used in the book are not the true identities of the clients from which they came. Any identification is probably not mere coincidence, but from the commonalities of being from an addicted home.

To Jack,
whom I dearly love

Contents

Preface ix

Acknowledgments xiii

Introduction 1

Chapter 1
Vignettes 7

Chapter 2
Roles 11

Chapter 3
Family Rules: Don't Talk, Don't Trust, Don't Feel 27

Chapter 4
Progression of the Roles 47

Chapter 5
Shame Circle 65

Chapter 6
Family Violence 85

Chapter 7
The Adult Child 105

Chapter 8
The Child within the Home 143

Chapter 9
Using Resources 173

Appendices 183
Problem Solving Form
Resources
Suggested Reading

About the Author 197

Preface

"I spent my whole life making sure I didn't end up like my dad. And now, the only difference between my dad and me is that my dad died from his alcoholism and I don't have to die from mine."

It has been twenty years since I first heard those words. In that time I have listened to similar stories repeated by men and women, young and old, across the world. Be it the alcoholic, the drug addict, the sex addict, or the gambler, they were raised with chemical dependency, substance abuse, or other addictive disorders. Every one of them had said to themselves, *it will never happen to me.* They were going to make sure they did not do what their parents had done. As I sit in family groups, I hear the same story from husbands, wives, and partners. They, too, have been raised in addictive families and have repeated those same words. In their wildest dreams, they didn't imagine it could ever happen to them. But they married alcoholics—some for a second or third time—even though the words *it will never happen to me* were thought and spoken with all sincerity. Today they are all as surprised to see the cycle of addiction repeating itself as addicts and family members were many years ago, when I originally wrote *It Will Never Happen to Me.* It does not take long before their children are also echoing those same words. And while adult-age children today are more able to identify that they were raised with addiction, they are still just as impacted by it. Another generation of young children continues to have to fight for esteem amidst chaos and fear.

My work and personal life are guided by the belief that no one deserves to live with fear and shame. I was raised in a family setting where addiction was a way of life. Aside from my father being alcoholic, we lived in a small town where my parents owned a tavern that was central to our logging community. Chronic drinking among adults was common to most and exposure to this was the norm. Unbeknownst to my mother, my father's drinking was well established prior to their marriage. He was just twenty-two years of age, she was seventeen. Having been raised with alcoholism and compulsive gambling, the earlier stages of my father's addictive behavior were not concerns for my mother.

It would be in growing up with an established legacy and an entrenched addictive family that I would find my way into what was then referred to as the "alcoholism field." I loved my parents dearly as I knew they loved me. Notwithstanding, I experienced a family wreaked with havoc by the emotional, physical, and spiritual ravages of addiction.

Over twenty years ago when I was asked to create a family program in a small chemical dependency unit of a hospital, I didn't know to ask questions. I assumed when I was asked to develop family programming that "family" meant "children." So I began to invite children into the program to talk about their experiences. My clients in the 1970s were of the age that many had adult-age children who were no longer living in the home. I believed, however, that if they had grown up with ten, fifteen, or twenty years of alcoholism they deserved to have a chance to talk about that experience. Growing up in my family I had learned to be hypervigilant to the expressed and the unexpressed, and so I was a good listener. I expected these adult-age children would talk freely and I would be of some service by listening. They came, but they didn't seem to know what to say. They struggled with their thoughts and feelings. Most would tell me how well they were doing, how they hoped their parent(s) would get better, but that they didn't really have any needs of their own. And certainly, it would never happen to them. Most were still caught up in the delusion that they had not been seriously impacted by the addiction.

It was in this context I first began to use the phrase "adult child." From a practical standpoint it defined who I was working with, the preteen, the adolescent, or the adult child in the family. It also acknowledged and validated that this adult was carrying the pain of his or her childhood vulnerabilities, having spent life masking and defending against the effects of a troubled family.

Then there were the teenagers. They were very concerned for others in their family, but in their minds they certainly didn't need to talk about themselves. Or they were angry and had an attitude that said they were doing just fine without me or anybody else.

Lastly, were the younger children, and here is where I found honesty and truth.

Before me I witnessed a continuum so blatant and yet so unseen it would ignite in me a need to look deeper within and into those with whom I was working. It is from those early experiences the first edition of *It Will Never Happen to Me* was written.

This was a time when saying out loud, "I was raised in an alcoholic home" brought gasps from people. It was before the days of media exposure. To discuss family problems, let alone to name addiction, was perceived by families as a major act of shame and betrayal.

Since those years, several changes have occurred to make it possible for families affected by addiction to break the cycle of their family history. There are many books on recovery available in bookstores compared to the days when not one book could be located. *It Will Never Happen to Me* has two million copies in print. It has been translated into five different languages ranging from Japanese to Swedish. Twelve Step groups permeate rural and urban America and are found throughout the world. Mental health specialists, family service agencies, and educational professionals are much more aware of and prepared to address the implications of addiction. Family secrets are much more openly talked about.

Yet, for most children growing up with addiction today, the experiences are very similar to the days of the past. They live with fear, loneliness, and confusion. Many continue to witness or experience direct physical or sexual abuse. They fear talking about what is happening and are learning to deny, rationalize, and tolerate the hurtful. Their lives are just as isolated as those of children twenty years ago, and as a consequence, the long-range impact for the child has not changed, unless there has been some type of direct intervention. Adult children continue to become addicted, marry addicts, and become depressed and rageful. They often do this as they push to excel and overachieve educationally and materially.

As you read, do so to understand, not to feel guilt or blame. This book is meant to offer a foundation for understanding what occurred growing up in an addictive family and to offer hope for recovery. With this in mind, know that a person does not make a conscious decision about becoming an addict or a coaddict. Without the intrusion of addiction, he or she would have made other choices.

Many readers will find *It Will Never Happen to Me* a catalyst that provokes a multitude of feelings. These feelings may be painful. I urge you to share your feelings. For too long family members have suffered in silence.

Let me close by acknowledging the resiliency in all of us who grew up with addiction. Irrespective of how we have been negatively impacted, each and every one of us has incredible strengths. It is my hope you will draw on the strengths and be open to the fact that one's pride in survivorship needs to extend beyond the ability to survive and embrace the right to thrive.

I also want to acknowledge each and every one of you who have ever thought, spoken, believed, and hoped *it will never happen to me.* Because of that conviction, and because of your impact on me, together we have the possibility of creating a different journey for ourselves and others.

Acknowledgments

Many people have helped to make this book a reality. Over the years, I have received support from a multitude of professional and personal friends. Yet the greatest motivator has continued to be the many young and adult children who shared parts of their lives with me. Their courage, vulnerability, and honesty inspired me on all levels. It is those lives that give the emotional depth and incredibly rich meaning to *It Will Never Happen to Me.* This book has been written in honor of each and every one who has traveled on this healing journey.

While I have had strong support from so many, there is a group of people who have been more directly involved in the creating of *It Will Never Happen to Me.* A special thank-you to Renee Cavalier, Joan Fiset, and Jane Middleton Moz for their poetry and Peter Nardi for his story. Your words, written many years ago, have offered validation and hope for the journey.

Victoria Danzig, Martha Ranson, Margaret Hillman, Lynn Sanford, Jael Greenleaf, Deborah Parker, and Muriel Zink played a direct role in the first edition, giving their support and feedback to me, and continue to be a significant part of my life.

Bob Stein, Annie Doce, Bary Levy, and Anne Marie Piontek—you will not be forgotten for your original contributions.

Sandi Klein, my assistant, you have been an invaluable help for which I am grateful.

It Will Never Happen to Me is truly my child, a very special child. I can offer it only because of the important people in my life. While many of them have already been acknowledged, I need to add to this list my grandmother Margaret Dolquist, a lifelong mentor, who passed away just a couple of years ago at the age of ninety-seven. My long-standing friends Shelia Fields and Lori Dwinell, your unconditional support of me has always been most valued. I am grateful for the friendships of Bob Martin, Mary Carol Melton, and Sis Wenger. I have been blessed with their validation and enthusiasm for my writings and work. A special thanks as well to my friends Ginny Brown and Russel Zink—angels who are always there to remind me to take care of me.

Since the original edition, my father and childhood friend Debbie have died from their addictions. I would like to acknowledge the incredible meaning and gifts they gave me in their life.

Tammy Stark worked for me for over thirteen years. Her life passion was in her dedication to the readers of my many books. She believed wholeheartedly in the recovery journey that would lie ahead. While invisible to most by name, and now having passed away, may she be remembered for her commitment to the many readers.

Since the original writing, I have been quite visible to the world. During that time, my mother and sister, Jana, would continue in their ongoing support. While my work would lead me to share about my personal life, which would reflect upon theirs, they have stood with me in pride and love. Thank you. Let me thank my stepfather, Tom, as well. You are such a light in our lives.

As said in the original edition, there is no other person I am more indebted to than Jack Fahey, my husband, for the fact this book exists. He was there for the gnashing of teeth that came with the many rewrites, the emotional pain that was tapped attempting to speak to the vulnerability of living with addiction, and the joy in witnessing the journey into recovery.

Thank you all.

Introduction

While hundreds of thousands of people are in recovery from chemical dependency, codependency, and adult child issues, our communities continue to be impacted by addiction. Heroin, cocaine, crystal methamphetamine, and marijuana use is rampant throughout our communities. But historically, the number one abused drug is alcohol.

Today, compared to the time of the writing of the first edition of *It Will Never Happen to Me,* we seldom refer to someone as alcoholic and recognize that if people are addicted they are often addicted to more than one substance. We use phrases like "chemically dependent" or "addict" to recognize that irrespective of the predominant substance addiction, they need to refrain from the use of alcohol and other drugs. This has occurred for two reasons. The first being it was recognized that many alcoholics were actively addicted to at least one other substance. Secondly, that even if they did not show signs of a second addiction, they needed to refrain from the use of other substances because those other substances would often lead them to relapse in their alcoholism or to engage in a second addiction. For these reasons, the words "alcoholic," "addict," and "chemically dependent" will be used interchangeably throughout this book.

When these terms are used within this book, they are referring to people who have neither the ability to consistently control their drinking or using, nor the capability to predict their behavior once they start to drink or use. Their drinking/using causes problems in major areas of their lives and yet they continue to do so. This is a person who has developed a psychological dependency on a substance coupled with a physiological addiction. It is someone who has experienced a change in tolerance to alcohol/drugs and needs to drink/use more to acquire the desired effect. Their need to drink or use becomes a greater and greater preoccupation in their lives. At one time in their lives, they had the ability to choose to drink or use. In time, it became not a matter of choice, but a compulsion.

Many people are confused about chemical dependency because there is no one specific pattern of behavior. Addicts differ in their styles of drinking/using and the consequences of the addiction widely vary. Some drink daily; others in episodic patterns; some stay dry for long intervals between binges; some drink enormous quantities of alcohol and use other drugs, while others do not. Some drink only beer; some drink only wine; while for others the choice is hard liquor. Still others will drink a wide variety of alcoholic beverages. Although addiction appears very early in the lives of some people, for others it takes years to develop. Some claim to have started drinking addictively from their first drink; many others report they drank for years before crossing over the "invisible line" that separates social drinking from addictive drinking.

While the focus of this book will remain on homes where alcohol is the primary drug, it is my hope the reader will see similarities in other substance-abusing families. The commonalities will be in living with extremes, living with the unknown, or living with the fears. It is the living in a system where the addiction has become central to the family and the needs of the individual family members become secondary to the needs of the addict and his or her addiction.

Commonalities

Since the original writing we have not only been more adept at recognizing multidrug abuse, we are recognizing what is referred to as process addictions and the fact that both substance and process addictions often coexist and may be interrelated. Such addictions would include gambling, spending, eating disorders, sex, love, and relationship addictions. The commonalities across addictive disorders are:

1. A pattern of out-of-control behavior, meaning that they are not able to predict their use once they engage in the substance or behavior, nor willingly stop their use
2. Negative consequences due to the behavior
3. Inability to stop, despite the consequences
4. An increase in tolerance and amounts of indulgence—the need to use or engage more to get the desired effect

5. Preoccupation—the anticipation of, involvement in, or reflection about their addictive behavior is the focus of their thoughts and feelings
6. Denial—minimization, rationalization, denial of their behavior as a problem permeates their thinking to the point of delusional thinking

Addictive obsession can exist in whatever generates significant mood alteration, whether it is the self-nurturing of food, the excitement of gambling, or the intoxication of alcohol or other drugs.

Coaddiction

Irrespective of the substance or object of the addiction, the behavior of the coaddicted parent follows very common routes as well. In the earlier writing, spouses and partners of the alcoholic were referred to as coalcoholics. Today they are more commonly thought of as codependents, or coaddicts. Originally the prefix "co" was used to describe a marriage partner who had become increasingly preoccupied with the behavior of the addict and functioned in the role of a primary enabler. It now encompasses the dynamics of giving up a sense of self, or experiencing a diminished sense of self in reaction to an addictive system.

Typically the codependent (or coaddict) experience involves:

1. Loss of sense of self, how they feel, and what they need
2. Being obsessed with another person who facilitates not dealing with own life
3. Reacting to someone else's behavior instead of acting from personal motives
4. Being all-consumed with another and putting own priorities on hold
5. Taking responsibility for other people, tasks, and situations
6. Engaging in a denial system

For children in the family, the combination of addiction and coaddiction results in neither parent being responsive and available on a consistent, predictable basis. Children are affected not only by the addicted parent, but also by the nonaddicted parent (if there is one) and by the unhealthy family dynamics created as a consequence of living in an addictive system.

Children

As of 2001, the National Association of Children of Alcoholics has reported 76 million Americans, about 43 percent of the U.S. adult population, have been exposed to alcoholism in the family. Almost one in five adult Americans (18 percent) lived with an alcoholic while growing up. There are an estimated 26.8 million children of alcoholics in the United States. Preliminary research suggests that over 11 million of these children are under the age of eighteen. Compared to children of nonalcoholics:

- They are more at risk for alcoholism and other drug abuse.
- They are more likely to marry into families in which alcoholism is prevalent.

We also recognize clinically that as adults, they experience a subset of behaviors related to shame-based beliefs that create depression, victimization, rage, and a lack of meaning in their lives. While children from difficult environments often show much resiliency, for many, it is at a very high price.

One of the gifts of what we have come to learn about people raised in chemically dependent families is that it has offered extremely useful information for people raised in other types of troubled families as well. Whether or not you were raised in an addictive family system, *It Will Never Happen to Me* may very well offer a framework to understand your situation. We have long recognized that people raised with physical and sexual abuse strongly identify as if they were raised with addiction. People raised with mental illness, ranging from schizophrenia to depression, to raging parents, frequently identify with adult child issues. People raised with parents affected by chronic health issues or physical challenges, as well as those raised by an adult child who may not manifest an addiction but whose thinking and behavior is often characteristic of an addict, may also identify. The connecting thread between these different types of families is experiencing chronic loss that fuels emotional isolation, rigidity, or shame.

Whatever the circumstances, when you come from a history of loss, it is like being a first cousin to the person raised with addiction. Therefore, if this information can benefit others raised in troubled families, this is an added gift.

Chapter 1

Vignettes

BELIEFS:
- No matter what I do it is never good enough
- Something bad is going to happen

I remember, as a boy, coming home from school and seeing either the living-room or the dining-room furniture thrown out in the driveway. It would startle me—actually it would blow my mind. My first thought would be to get it back in the house before anyone else would see it, and we (my mom or brothers) would get it back into the house. I would feel slightly relieved. However, for several days, or maybe a week or two, depending on the severity of the act, I would be caught up in the thought of what would happen next, such as Would my dad give something of ours away to a stranger? *And he did give away things we liked a lot, like a pair of skis, a rifle, and once our dog. He would tell us he hated us, or he would call us worthless so-and-so's. I would always ponder those incidents; reflecting now, I spent years worrying about Dad's well-being, or how I could help him. Why did he do those things? What did I do? What did we do? What could I do to make him different? I went from a young boy to a young man with my thoughts, alone, socially and mentally. I never got to know myself, and I guess I still don't. I am still a loner, I don't know how to live, to have fun, or to enjoy life.*

—Bill T.

BELIEFS:
- I am responsible for other people's behavior
- There must be something wrong with me

My father is an alcoholic. He has never admitted to that fact. He and my mom used to get in lots of fights when I lived at home. The six of us kids were used as pawns in their war games. I always wondered whether or not I was responsible for his drinking. When the fights were going on, I always retreated to my room. There I felt secure. Now, I am twenty-two and have been married for two years. I have this affliction that whenever the slightest thing happens I always say I am so sorry. I am sorry when the milk is not cold, sorry that the wet towel was left in the gym bag. I just want to take the blame for everything, even things I have no control over.

—Sharon R.

BELIEFS:
- Other people's needs are more important than my own
- It is not okay to ask for help

I am a twenty-nine-year-old woman (girl actually) who is the only child of two chemically dependent parents. When I was little, I was lonely and afraid most of the time. But when the rest of your friends seem normal and carefree, and your parents are into their own set of problems, whom do you tell those things to? When I used to be awakened by my parents arguing, I longed to have a sister to talk to. Somehow I always felt if I had a sister to mother, to make things all right, that I would have felt better. I never once thought about someone mothering me or making me feel better. My parents separated when I was in sixth grade, and I continued to live with my father. I was relieved when my mother left, because at least then, the fighting stopped. But then things kind of got turned around and I found myself being the parent and my father the child. I prided myself on the way I was brought up because I thought it made me strong, independent, and self-reliant. Now that I am older, I am so angry I feel like screaming at someone—but there is no one left to scream at. My father died in 1970, and at that time, I guess my mother just gave up and proceeded to drink herself to death. Well, now I am almost thirty and my drinking has increased; I know it and at the same time I don't want to stop. I enjoy it. It helps me to loosen up and feel better. I started therapy last year. My therapist told me I drink to ease the pain. Maybe that is true. I never even thought about being in pain. The scary part is I seem to be emulating the very behavior and role models I shouldn't. But where do you go to undo twenty years of a life-patterning style?

—Barbara P.

Chapter 2
Roles

"We became the late-night regulars at the local hospital's emergency room. For instance, one night Mom dropped a gin bottle on her foot and sliced one of her tendons. Another time she was washing dishes drunk, broke a glass, and sliced a tendon in her arm. Another night she threw a saltshaker at Dad, got him in the forehead, and he needed stitches. Once when I was alone with Mom, she fell through the window and was lying there in blood and broken glass, half on the patio, half in the family room. I phoned Dad and he yelled at me to pull her in from the window so she wouldn't fall farther and slice herself in half. I got down on my hands and knees in the broken glass. I stuck myself through the hole she'd fallen through and moved enough glass away from her so I could pull her inside without cutting her up too badly. Then I cleaned her off and waited for Dad."

—Jan

Somebody may ask, "What happened then?" Nothing happens then. Nothing. It is Tuesday night. Or it could be Wednesday, or maybe Thursday. But nothing in particular happens.

But something does happen—children learn to repress their fears, sadness, anger, and humiliation. Yet somewhere in their bodies the depth of those experiences and feelings remains, typically dictating how they will perceive and respond to themselves and others. They walk through life conditioned by years of helplessness and powerlessness. Eighteen-year-old Jan is already abusing alcohol and cocaine, is bulimic, sexually promiscuous, and ultimately suicidal.

While the following experience may not be as extreme, Bill would also experience the consequences of living in an addictive family.

"We didn't know Dad was addicted to drugs or alcohol until my parents separated. My mom kept it a secret, and my dad just didn't come home

much. He was a doctor and we thought all doctors worked a lot. When he was home we were to stay out of his way, not to be a problem. We learned to never question and never expect anything. We were just supposed to accept his absence and disregard for us. Mom vacillated between depression, being supermother, and having a short temper. We could see her stress but it was never discussed. I really thought I was not affected but then I began to have problems in my relationships. I always seemed to need one but didn't know how to be close. I became anxious about everything and then that would end the relationship and sabotage my performance at school. I began to experience depression and still struggle with it today. I realize I missed out on a whole lot of basics, such as feeling I was worthy or that my needs were of value or that I could talk about any of it."

While it is true children growing up with addiction are at high risk to become addicted to substances, it is also common to see that they may modify their addiction to a different substance or process than the one they were raised with, such as eating disorders, sex addiction, money-related or work addictions. They frequently marry someone who also has an addictive disorder. In addition, a common emotional theme for adult children is difficulty in identifying and expressing feelings; they are often rigid in their behavior and highly controlling of people, places, and things. Some find themselves overly dependent on others. As in Bill's situation, they may feel no sense of power or choice in the way they live. A pervasive sense of fear and guilt often exists in their lives. Many experience depression and frequently lack the ability to feel close or intimate with another human being.

As complex as the outcomes are for many children, healing can begin by understanding the basics of the addictive family system.

Reacting to the Troubled Family System

While one of the clearest indicators of a smoothly working family is consistency, the words that best describe living in a chemically dependent family are "inconsistency" and "unpredictability." It is my belief that what a spouse or child does while living in an addictive environment, they do because at that time it made sense to them. As the problems surrounding the addiction cause more and more inconsistency and unpredictability in the home, the behavior of the nonaddicted family members typically becomes an attempt to restabilize the family system. Members of this family system act and react in a manner that makes life easier and less painful.

In most well-functioning families, one finds emotions being expressed clearly, with each person being given the opportunity to share his or her feelings. Emotions are accepted by an attentive group that offers understanding and support. Family members can freely ask for attention, and in return give attention to others.

In a home beset with addiction, emotions are repressed and become twisted. Emotions are often not shared, and unfortunately when they are expressed, it is done in a judgmental manner with blame being placed on one another.

> *"Everyone was worrying about someone else's feelings and discounting their own. My mother would feel sad and worry about something going on with me. Rather than see it as my mother's sadness and worry, my father wanted me to be different so she wouldn't feel sad or worry. No one wanted to take responsibility for their own problems—they always blamed someone else."*

While constructive alliances are part of the healthy family, adult members of an addicted family system often lack alliance. If alliances are demonstrated, they are destructive and usually consist of one parent and a child (or children) against the other parent.

Families have rules, which need to be fair and flexible. These rules also need to be verbalized. Rules such as "No hitting" or "Everyone will have a chance to be heard" lead to healthier functioning within a system. In addictive family structures, rules are usually fueled by shame, guilt, or fear. Rather than a verbalized rule which says, "There will be no hitting," there is an unspoken, silent rule, which says, "You won't tell others how you got that bruise."

Many times, there are clearly defined roles within the family. It is typical for adults in the family to divide or share the roles of being breadwinner and administrator—the one who makes the decisions within the home. Children raised in homes where open communication is practiced and consistency of lifestyle is the norm usually have the ability to adopt a variety of roles, dependent upon the situation. These children learn how to be responsible, to organize, develop realistic goals, play, laugh, and enjoy themselves. They learn a sense of flexibility and spontaneity. They are usually taught how to be sensitive to the feelings of others and are willing to be helpful. These children learn a sense of autonomy and how to belong to a group. Children growing up in addictive homes, however, seldom learn the combinations of roles that mold healthy personalities. Instead, they become locked into roles based on their perception of what they need to do to "survive" and bring stability to their lives.

Looking Good

School counselors and employees in juvenile justice systems and family service agencies often report contact with a high percentage of children from addicted homes. But, they are more apt to describe the youngster known as the "acting-out" child, and not the majority of children in chemically dependent families. I contend most children in chemically dependent families are *not* seen by school counselors, are *not* addressed in juvenile justice systems and family service agencies. They are not necessarily the children who become runaways, fill our juvenile justice systems, or perform poorly in school. They aren't always the ones who have adjustment problems, nor are they blatantly angry. The majority have strong tendencies to appear "normal" and to be from "typical" American families. They do not exhibit problematic behavior and rarely, if ever, talk about the addiction in their primary family. While there are a substantial number of problematic children, the majority of children raised in addiction do not draw enough attention to themselves to be identified as being in need of special attention. As a result, they are a neglected population. If they are busy and look good, they will be ignored.

Feeling trapped in a highly confusing system, family members do what is needed to be safe. They do what they need to preserve the family system. This typically means they hide their feelings behind an artificial behavior pattern.

The majority of children tend to adopt one or a combination of the following three roles: the *responsible child*, the *adjuster*, or the *placater*. These are roles that allow children to draw either positive attention or no attention to themselves. A smaller percentage finds ways to draw negative attention by adopting a fourth role, the *acting-out child*. Some children may clearly fit into one or more of these four roles. For most, though, there is a primary role and then secondary roles. Some switch roles. What is important is to identify first the strength and then the vulnerabilities of each role.

An only or oldest child is most likely to be a very *responsible child*. This child not only assumes a great deal of responsibility for himself, but does so for other family members as well. This is the nine-year-old going on thirty-five, the twelve-year-old going on forty. From the onset of addiction in the family, this child has been an adult. It is the seven-year-old putting Mom to bed, the nine-year-old getting dinner ready every night, the twelve-year-old driving Dad around because Dad's too drunk to drive himself, or simply the child whose adultlike behavior is compensating for a parent's immaturity. This role is one in which the child seldom misbehaves but, rather, takes on many of the household and parenting responsibilities for the other siblings and, very possibly, for the parents.

Next is the child who is usually not the oldest or the only child. This is the child who does not develop the need to be responsible for himself or others. The need is not as great because there is often an older sibling providing the needed structure in the environment. This middle or younger child finds the best role for him to play is that of the *adjuster*. For him, it is easier to simply follow directions, handle whatever has to be handled, and adjust to the circumstances of the day. This coping pattern allows the child to appear more flexible, more spontaneous, and possibly, more selfish than others in the home.

A third common pattern within this increasingly chaotic home life is that of the *placater.* This is the family comforter, or otherwise known as the household social worker. It is this child who often tries to make others in the home feel better, as if he or she is responsible for whatever pain the family is experiencing. This youngster is extremely sensitive to other people's feelings and does what he or she can to lessen the intensity of the pain within the home. The placater is a good listener, taking away Mom's sadness, brother's fear, sister's embarrassment, and Dad's anger.

We can easily find value in all of these role characteristics and typically don't see them as destructive. In fact, labeling children with words such as "responsible," "caring," and "able to adjust to crisis" allows them, as adults, to pat themselves on the back for having been such good "survivors." The survival mechanisms of those who "look good" often lead to unhealthy extremes. Such unusual development of coping behavior often results in emotional and psychological deficits. It is the understanding of such deficits that allows one to understand how survivors end up living out a family script. It is this family script that draws them into behaving addictively themselves, marrying someone who is or becomes an addict, or having an unusual number of problems in their adult years.

While most children react to the turmoil in their lives in a way that doesn't draw negative attention to them or their family members, a small number of them find ways to say loudly that something is very wrong. Metaphorically and literally, they walk through their adolescence and, often, adult years, with their fists clenched and raised, with a finger protruding, saying, "There is something very wrong in my life and you are going to notice me." Instead of behaving in a manner that actually brings greater stability into their lives, or at least one that does not add to the turmoil, *acting-out children*—the fourth common role—often display delinquent problematic behavior. Their behavior more adequately typifies the true state of the family.

As you read further, do not be locked into the labels of these roles. There are many possible adjectives that may have more meaning for you. Common terms may be "hero," "scapegoat," "comic," "wallflower," "scorekeeper," "peacemaker," and so on. What is most crucial is to ascertain if you identify with any particular role (named by me or you) as a part of responding to an addictive family and to ultimately recognize both its strengths and vulnerabilities.

The Responsible Child

"Everything must be in order in my household or it brings great anxiety to me. The orderliness probably stems from the chaos I felt in my adolescent years. My parents' house was always physically orderly, but human relationship was CHAOS."

Children need consistency and structure. As a chemically dependent person progresses into their addiction, and the codependent becomes more and more preoccupied with the addict, children experience decreasing consistency and structure in the family unit. This makes their lives less and less predictable. Some days when Dad is drinking, no disruption or tension occurs. On other days he becomes loud, opinionated, and demanding in his expectations of the children. Mom at times reacts to this disruptive behavior by being passive and ignoring it, while other times she makes arrangements for the children to go to the neighbors' until Dad goes to bed, or tells them to go outside and play. The children don't know what to expect from either parent when Dad drinks.

When the parents do not provide structure and consistency, children will find ways to provide it for themselves. The oldest child, or an only child, very often becomes the *responsible* one in the family. This child takes responsibility for the environmental structure in the home and provides consistency for others. When Dad becomes verbally abusive while drinking, this youngster gathers the coats and pajamas of the other children and heads them to the neighbor's home. While Mom and Dad are out drinking together, the responsible one directs the other children to their bedrooms, ensures they complete their homework, instructs them to change into their nightclothes and go to bed. This is the nine-year-old girl who has a flowchart across her bedroom wall marking what she needs to do on a daily basis to take care of the house. She assumes a lot of responsibility because she feels the need for structure. In this situation, she perceives that her mother, who works more than eight hours a day, is always sad and tired. Mom never complains, but this young girl knows it helps when the rugs are vacuumed, the dirty clothes ready for the laundry, the shopping completed, the dishes washed, and the ironing finished. She also knows everything seems better when her brothers and sisters receive direction from her about where they can and cannot go; they feel safer. They are less apt to bother Mom and Dad. Overall, everyone in the family seems a lot happier.

Sometimes the responsible children are directed to assume this role; other times, they assume the role voluntarily. One woman, age thirty, said, "My mom took me out of a foster home I had been in for six years just so I could be home to take care of my two younger brothers." Another adult woman told me, "My being such a good homemaker and parent to my sister made it easier for Dad to be out of the house when Mom was drinking. He didn't know what to do, so he just worked later and later and had more and more business trips." It is typical for the chemically dependent and codependent parent to take great pride in their adultlike youngsters. Responsible children make life easier for the parents by providing more time for the addicted parent to be preoccupied with drinking and for the codependent to be preoccupied with their partner.

Whether responsible children are blatantly directed into this role or more subtly fall into it, it is a role that brings them comfort. Playing the responsible role provides stability in the life of this oldest or only child and in the lives of other family members. Responsible children feel, and are, very organized. They practice this role so consistently that they become very adept at planning and manipulating. In order to provide the structure they seek they often manipulate their brothers and sisters. This ability to organize, to affect others, and to accomplish goals provides these children with leadership qualities—qualities that get them elected as class leaders, captains of teams, and so forth.

Responsible youngsters become adept at setting tangible goals: "I'll be sure I get the grocery list done tonight and do the shopping tomorrow after school" and "I'll be sure the boys get their baths tonight, and the girls tomorrow night." These goals are realistic and attainable. In an addictive home, one is most realistic if one thinks of goals on a short-range basis. "What can I get done today?" "What will I get done tomorrow?" If these children begin thinking about what they want to accomplish in terms of the next few weeks, or months, they know that their home situation may not remain stable enough for them to follow through with their plans. Too many long-range plans are affected by whether or not the addicted parent is drinking. "I never planned a birthday party for myself. If I wanted a party, the best way to have one was to call Mom on my noon hour and ask her then. It always depended on Dad's mood, and she could only predict it a few hours ahead." So, in setting goals and making them realistic enough to be accomplished, the child feels good about himself. He achieves the goals and he experiences a sense of accomplishment.

Thus, responsibility, organization, setting and achieving goals are attributes encouraged and rewarded at home and school. Obviously this is not the kind of behavior that sees children being sent to school counselors, nor that which gets them punished by their parents.

These responsible children have learned to rely completely on themselves. It is what makes the most sense to them. They have learned the best way to achieve stability is to provide it for themselves: "If you want to get something done, do it yourself." They cannot consistently rely on Mom or Dad. The parents may respond to the children emotionally and psychologically at times, but the unpredictability and inconsistency of the parents' behavior are destructive elements.

Children also come to believe that other adults will not be available to them when help is needed. Typically, they believe most adults are not capable, nor astute, enough to provide any insight or direction for their personal lives. Youngsters interpret this to mean others don't care or aren't very sensitive. Such messages, internalized by the children, are possibly never consciously acknowledged.

Most grown-ups perceive responsible children as very mature, dependable, and serious. Peers often view these children as not quite so much fun as their other friends. These youngsters most typically either become active in structured social activities or do not have significant social lives. They need to be in organized situations where they feel in control and a sense of safety. Being goal-oriented allows them a diversion from the family pain. This provides them with psychological relief and they get positive feedback. Most importantly, at this time it does make their lives easier.

The Adjuster

"Put me in any situation now and I can adjust. But please, don't ask me to be responsible for it or change it."

When others in the home—typically an older sibling, or Mom or Dad—provide structure, younger children may find it is not necessary to be responsible for themselves. The child called the *adjuster* finds it much easier to exist in this increasingly chaotic family situation by simply adjusting to whatever happens. This youngster does not attempt to prevent or alleviate any situation. The child doesn't think about the situation or experience any emotions as a result of it. Whatever happens, when it happens, is simply handled. The adjuster's bottom-line thinking is "I can't do anything about it anyway," which in the child's mind seems to be a fairly realistic attitude. A clinician or a family therapist would describe the adjuster as the child who seems most detached from the family. The other children in the home may perceive this child as more selfish, while the parents don't seem to notice this child as much.

While the responsible child, the placater, and certainly the acting-out child are quite visible, the adjusting child is seen less often. This is the youngster who most likely goes to his room unannounced, who spends less time at home and more time with his friends; this is the family member who seems oblivious to the conflicts and emotions at home.

As the child heads out the door to stay at a friend's house for the night and Dad hollers, "Where do you think you're going? Who gave you permission to go anywhere? You aren't going anywhere. You are staying right here tonight!" the adjuster simply comes back, returns his clothes to the closet, and quietly calls his friend to give some excuse for not coming over. He knows that Dad had told him earlier in the day that it was okay to spend the night at his friend's house. He also knows it won't do any good to argue with Dad now that he has been drinking. This same child, when Dad hasn't shown up for one single ball game all season, simply tells Mom it was no big deal and not to feel bad because he doesn't feel bad. "Besides, if Dad had shown up, he probably would have been drunk anyway." It's just easier to accept the situation.

Children describe the many times Mom gets tired and angry with Dad because of his drinking, so she packs the children and their belongings into the car and races off to a relative's. The next day she packs them up again and returns home, because somehow Mom and Dad got things worked out. So there they are, back home the very next day. Their clothes are back in the drawers and they're all sitting at the dinner table—everyone acting as if the previous night didn't happen. So many have told me, "It doesn't help to question it. It is just easier that way. And, it certainly doesn't help to interfere." Adjusting children find it wiser to follow and simply not draw attention to themselves. This behavior is less painful for these children and makes life easier for the rest of the family as well. The role of the adjuster is permeated with denial, but without the focus on others. It is this lack of attention to others that makes adjusters appear to be more selfish.

Acting without thinking or feeling is typical of the true adjuster. A young woman once told me about the time she and her father had gone to a ball game together, thirty miles from home. She said her father dropped her off at the game, and he went to a tavern. He was intoxicated when he picked her up after the game. She said this didn't cause her any concern. In fact it was typical. But this night, as they headed for home, he stopped at another tavern, fifteen miles away. He gave her the keys to the car and said, "Now, I want you to drive home and tell your mom I am at the D.B. Tavern and I'll be home in a little while." The young girl got in the car and drove home. Even though she didn't know how to drive, she didn't question her father or his instructions. She said, "He had left the car running and it was an automatic. I just got in and pointed it toward home. I ran in and out of ditches and drove mostly on the shoulder, but I got home. I was crying the whole way home but when I got there I calmed myself down, went into the house, put the keys on the counter, walked into my mother's bedroom, told Mom that Dad was at the D.B. Tavern and would be home in a while. I then went to my room and went to bed." She said her father and mother both knew she didn't drive: her father ignored the fact; her mother didn't even ask how she got home. She said, "Once I got in the house, I didn't think about what had happened."

"Put me in any situation and I will handle it. I won't feel, get upset, or question it; I will just respond to it." The adjuster does not think of saying, "Dad, I can't drive home. I don't know how to drive." She doesn't want to upset Dad. She doesn't think of simply waiting for Dad to come back. After all, she was given instructions and she has learned the best way to keep peace in the family is to respond to those instructions without question. She doesn't think of calling her mother and asking for advice on how to handle the situation—she does not want to cause her mother any problems. It is just so much safer to handle the situation alone.

At school, the adjusting child is as nondescript as he or she is at home. Academically, this child is about average, not demonstrating brilliance or ignorance, consequently not drawing any negative or positive attention through schoolwork. As a consequence, this child does not greatly impact or impress teachers.

In social situations at school, the adjuster associates with other children but does not take any leadership roles. Rather, the adjuster remains somewhat detached and in the outer parameters of social circles.

The Placater

"Whenever a family problem comes up, both sides will call me to settle disputes. I am called on to make many decisions, and I do them all alone. Growing up, my friends used to ask me for advice as they felt that I 'knew' a lot and rarely had problems of my own."

In every home, there is usually at least one child who is particularly more sensitive—one who laughs and cries harder and seems to be more emotionally involved in everyday events. When parents talk about their children, it is typical to hear them identify one in particular as "the one who is more sensitive than the others." This is usually stated matter-of-factly and accepted as being quite normal. In the addicted family, the *placating* child is not necessarily the only sensitive child in the home, but is the one perceived as the "most sensitive." This child's feelings are hurt more easily than the others'. Yet, he likes to make others feel better. The placater finds the best way to cope in this inconsistent and tension-filled home is by acting in a way that will lessen his own tension and pain as well as that of the other family members. This child will spend his early and adolescent years trying to "fix" the sadness, fears, angers, and problems of brothers, sisters, and certainly, of Mom and Dad.

While Mom and Dad are arguing, and the other children are afraid of what will happen, the placater does something to diminish the fear. When a sibling is embarrassed by Mom's drunken behavior at the supermarket, this most sensitive child acts to make the situation less painful for the sister. A brother is angry because Dad broke another promise so this youngster reacts to help dispel the brother's anger. This pattern develops at a surprisingly young age, as demonstrated when five-year-old Michael told his crying mom, "Don't worry Mom, I won't remember all of this when I grow up." The placater is always there to make life easier for the others in the home.

As this sensitive child grows to adulthood, others experience him as a "nice" person. After all, he spends his time trying to please others, trying to make others feel better, and usually he succeeds in doing just that. The placater becomes very skilled at listening and demonstrating empathy and is well liked for these attributes. If this child is a full-fledged placater, he will never disagree. In fact, he is the first to apologize if he feels an apology is needed, especially if it will protect another person. Eleven-year-old Tom apologized to his mother on the average of ten to fifteen times a day. "I'm sorry you broke the milk bottle," "I'm sorry you don't feel well," "I'm sorry I am thirty seconds late to the breakfast table," "I am just plain sorry." Tom's mom was an addict, and Tom said to me, "I just couldn't figure out why she was always loaded and knew there must be something I did to make her so unhappy. So I just tried to make it better by apologizing."

Parents are often proud of the placater, believing he knows how to share. They know he is not a selfish child. They never have to worry about the placater being disappointed because he doesn't appear to get upset when plans fall through and he doesn't let anyone know he is bothered by anything. Dad doesn't take the children to the game as he promised; the placating youngster squelches his own disappointment and focuses on his younger brother for the rest of the day. When Mom says "No" unjustifiably, the sensitive child may have tears well up in his eyes, but he takes them to his room to cry alone. He isn't going to argue or run to the other parent. In every way he seems to be a very warm, caring, nonproblematic, sensitive child.

"By the time I was five I had learned how to take care of others. My parents repeatedly told me the story of what happened when I was in the hospital at age five for a tonsillectomy. While waiting in the 'pre-op' room, another five-year-old girl began to cry in anticipation of her surgery. I went to her and very expertly calmed and soothed her fear. In retrospect, I only did what I'd been trained for. That's what I did at home with my mother. I had to mask all of my own feelings in order to bring happiness to everyone else."

These characteristics of sensitivity are displayed outside the home just as they are within its walls. In fact these are the qualities that make the placating children so well liked by others. Acting the role of the placater is certainly safe for them. If they allowed themselves to risk self-disclosure, they would have to deal with their own reality and experience the pain of that reality. So these children are highly skilled at diverting attention from themselves and focusing it onto other persons. Imagine the resultant personality when this role is combined with that of the responsible child—the combination of the child responsible for the tangible environment and for the emotional needs of others. It is easy to understand why placaters are well liked at school and at home; it is even easier to recognize why they don't draw attention to themselves.

The Acting-Out Child

"Alcohol was uncool because that is what our parents used. So my friends and I started taking drugs. They could wipe out any feelings. I could decide what to feel. I felt relaxed, not so manic or intense. I took PCP in dosages even heroin addicts were afraid of and that made me feel powerful. People saw me as crazy but that was okay. I felt strong. Friends called me Loadie, and I wanted to wear that name as a star on my lapel. I looked up to my friends—they were fun, cool, and I wanted to be like them and liked by them. So I was off and running and never looking back."

The *acting-out* child is the assumed stereotype in an addictive family. They will cause disruption in their own lives and in the lives of other family members. In doing so, they will often provide distraction from the real issues.

If there is a delinquent child in the family, it is often easier for parents to focus on that child and the ensuing problems created rather than worry about Dad's or Mom's drinking or using. Such children are the ones who perform poorly or drop out of school, experience teenage pregnancy, drink at a preteen age, abuse other drugs, and exhibit other socially unacceptable behavior. They are also involved in the criminal justice system and end up admitted into psychiatric hospitals or other institutions.

While acting-out children are the ones most likely to be addressed and receive help from one or more professionals, the addiction within the family is typically ignored. Unacceptable behavior is learned, and parents are the primary role models in this learning process. Parents usually set the mold, either through action or inaction. Parental immaturity, often expressed in extreme selfishness, lack of consistency, cruel teasing, or inappropriate discipline, is frequently characteristic of life in addictive homes. Most children in trouble have an extremely poor self-image, reflecting the feeling they sense their parents have—inadequacy. Acting-out children find it nearly impossible to communicate their feelings to adults in a healthy way. While other children with the same problems learn how to repress problem areas and focus on other areas of their lives, acting-out children use unacceptable forms of behavior to say "Care about me" or "I can't cope." These children are attempting to be the voice for the family, saying, "Help! Look at us!" Often they have less denial than others about what is occurring in the family. They can be very creative and even show leadership ability. They just lead in the wrong direction.

Where other children tend to draw positive attention to themselves or escape attention, the acting-out child contributes to the severity of his own situation by eliciting the kind of attention that causes parents to cry, nag, belittle, or even strike their child. This ultimately undermines the child's developing self-esteem.

The opinions and acceptance of one's peers are extremely important to most teenagers. Children ascribing to roles in which they are preoccupied with the details of home or are emotionally detached have less concern for peer acceptance. The acting-out child, however, who lacks the ability to detach or focus on other things and lacks a strong parent-child relationship, will gravitate toward peers—peers who usually have equally low self-esteem.

Unfortunately, thousands of these acting-out children don't get help. For those who do, the help they get is only for their problematic behavior, not for being part of an addictive family system, which is the basis of their behavior.

Over the years, people have frequently asked how different these roles are from roles in other families. As said previously, frequently there are defined roles within any family as a result of parental expectations and the influence of birth order. The difference is that in the addictive family system the roles are fueled and created from a basis of fear and shame. As a result children become locked into them based on their perception of what is necessary for survivorship. Consequently, they rigidly adhere to the strength of a role to such an extreme that what was positive becomes a strong negative behavior. This is the result of not learning balance and the skills that come with a choice of role.

Whether or not you come from a shame-based family, the value of addressing roles is to recognize their strengths, vulnerabilities, and how they are integral to the family system.

The bottom line: *All children are affected.*

Chapter 3

Family Rules

Don't Talk, Don't Trust, Don't Feel

The Best Little Boy in the World (He Won't Tell) —Peter M. Nardi

Michael was doing very well in school. In fact, he was the brightest kid in class, the teacher's favorite, one of the best behaved. He never created any disciplinary problems and always hung out with the good crowd. The best little boy in the world. "Why can't we all be like Michael and sit quietly?" Sister Gertrude would say in her most melodious voice. Conform, be docile, do well, and be quiet. Hold it in. Don't tell a soul.

And now he was waiting at the school corner for his mother to pick him up. This was always the hardest moment. What will she look like, how will she sound? Michael could tell right away if she had been drinking. The muffled voice, the pale, unmade-up face. He really didn't know what it was all about. He just knew that when Dad came home he would fight with her. Argue, yell, scream, and run. Michael could hear them through the closed doors and over the humming of the air conditioner. He wondered if the neighbors could hear, too. Hold it in. Don't tell anyone.

He was still waiting at the corner. She was fifteen minutes late. It was so good to go to school and get out of the house. But when three o'clock came he would feel the tension begin to gather inside him. He never knew what to expect. When she was not drinking, she would be smiling, even pretty. When drunk, she'd be cold, withdrawn, tired, unloving, and not caring. Michael would cook dinner and straighten up the house. He would search for the alcohol, like egg-hunting on Easter morning, under the stuffed chair in the bedroom, in the laundry bag concealed among the towels, behind her hats in the closet. When he found it, he'd pour it down the sink drain. Maybe then no one would know that she'd been drinking. Maybe no one would fight. Don't tell a soul.

She still hadn't come to pick him up yet. She'd never been thirty minutes late. Sometimes she'd sleep late in the morning after Dad had already left for work, and Michael would make breakfast for his little sister and himself. Then a friend's mother would take them to school. The biggest problem was during vacation time, especially around the holidays. He wanted to play with his friends. But he was afraid to bring them home. He was afraid to go out and play, too, because then she would drink. Michael didn't want to be blamed for that. So he stayed in and did his homework and read. He didn't tell his friends. Hold it in.

And still he was waiting alone on the corner. Forty-five minutes late. Michael decided to walk the ten blocks home. He felt that he was old enough now. After all, he took care of his little sister a lot. He took care of his mother a lot. He was responsible. He always did what people told him to do. Everyone could count on him for help. Everyone did. And he never complained. Never fought, never argued, never yelled. The best little boy in the world. Hold it in.

When he got nearer to home Michael's heart felt as if it were going to explode. Her car was there. The house was locked tight. He rang the bell. He rang and rang as he felt his stomach turn inside out. He climbed through a window. No one seemed to be home. He looked around the house, in all the right hiding places. Finally, in the closet in his own bedroom, he saw his mom in her slip, with a belt around her neck and attached to the wooden rod. She was just sitting there, sobbing. She had been drinking. But maybe no one would find out. Michael wouldn't tell anyone, ever. Hold it in.

Family Rules

Thousands of children like Michael are being, or have been, raised in homes where at least one parent is chemically dependent. And like Michael, these children appear to suffer no apparent ill effects. These young people usually do not leave home prematurely. They are typical in that, like most children, they leave home at the ages of seventeen, eighteen, or nineteen. When they do venture out on their own, they face the task of making decisions about work, careers, lifestyles, friends, where and with whom they are going to live, and possibly, whether or not to enter a branch of the military. They also make decisions about marriage and whether or not to have children.

These children, along with thousands of other young people, are beginning to make some of the most important decisions of their lives and then spend years implementing those choices. Typically, it will take the next six to eight years to implement and follow through with these career and family decisions. During this time, young adults focus on external events. It is not normally a time when they sit back and contemplate how good or poor the past years were for them. If they recognize they grew up with addiction, they breathe a sigh of relief and pat themselves on the back for having survived. They then begin going about their own lives, yet they frequently stay socially and emotionally entangled with their family.

It is about this time, when a young person reaches the mid-twenties, that the effects of growing up in an addictive home become apparent. These now adult children begin to experience a sense of loneliness that doesn't make sense to them. They become aware of feelings that separate them from others and often may find themselves depressed. And while this depression occurs more frequently and lasts longer, the source of the depression seems unidentifiable. Feelings of fear and anxiousness occur more frequently but they don't know why they are having these feelings. They often feel empty and have difficulty maintaining close relationships. Many report that something seems to be missing in their relationships. A lack of meaningfulness begins to permeate every aspect of their lives. For many the repetition of the addiction has begun. Their drinking and using has become an important part of their life, or they are engaging in other behaviors in an addictive compulsive style, such as work, spending, and gambling, or they have disordered relationships with food. Or they find themselves in relationships with others who are engaging in addictive behaviors. Should any of this be occurring, their rationalizing and defending is blocking the ability to see this as a problem.

To break this cycle it is necessary to recognize the many processes that have occurred.

Don't Talk

> The Family Law: DON'T TALK ABOUT THE REAL ISSUES. The real issues: Mom is drinking again. Dad didn't come home last night. I had to walk home from school because Mom had passed out at home and forgot to come and get me. Dad was drunk at the ball game.
>
> Some say it is a rule; I believe, for most addictive families, it has become law. As one nine-year-old daughter said, *"When you have a rule in your house for so long, to not talk about Dad's drinking, it's r-e-a-l-l-y hard to talk now—even when he is sober."*

In the earlier stages of chemical dependency, when someone's drinking or using seems to become a more noticeable problem, family members usually attempt to rationalize the behavior. They begin to invent excuses: "Well, your dad has been working hard these past few months," or, "Your mom has been lonely since her best friend moved away." As the drinking or using increases, the rationalizations become their "normal" way of life. Family members focus on the problems but do not connect them to the addiction. An excuse offered to a child I had been working with for her dad's irrational (alcoholic) behavior was that he had a brain tumor and was going to die. The mother told the children their father wanted them to hate him before he died so it would be easier for them to accept his death when it happened. This now adult person explains, "It didn't feel right, but who was I to question my mom? She had enough problems as it was." As a child, this woman believed her father was going crazy. She felt his going crazy seemed more likely than that he was going to die from a tumor. She now understands that while her father acted crazy, his erratic behavior was due to his drinking. His increasingly controlling and tyrannical moods, his inconsistent behavior related to his blackouts, as well as his hallucinations, added to his appearance of craziness.

It is often easier to invent reasons, rather than naming chemical dependency, for crazy behavior. Should the drinking or using take place outside of the home and Dad doesn't act falling-down drunk or in a stupor when he comes home, or if they don't see him when he comes home, the children may more readily accept what Mom tells them—drinking is not the problem.

Children are like adults in that they, too, will believe addicts are homeless men or street junkies without jobs or families. If children do not understand addiction, it is difficult for them to identify their parent as chemically dependent.

Sandy said she knew her father wasn't alcoholic because, "My dad loved me and I knew that." No one ever explained to her that alcoholic people are also capable of loving others. She believed because her father loved her he could not be alcoholic. Sandy had heard about alcoholism only once at church where a recovering alcoholic told his story. But what she heard was that particular person's story of his drinking. She could not relate this story to her father. Her father certainly didn't sound, look, or behave like this man. Such fragmented information is typical of children's lack of knowledge concerning chemical dependency.

Another way family members rationalize the erratic behavior is not to discuss or in any manner talk about what's really happening at home. Thirteen-year-old Steve said, "I thought I was going crazy. I thought I was the only one in my house who knew Dad was an alcoholic. I didn't know anyone else knew." I asked him why he believed this to be true. He answered, "Because no one else ever said anything." Steve described an incident that occurred when he and his father were at home alone. In a semiconscious state from drunkenness, his father had fallen, hit his head on the coffee table, thrown up, and was on the floor bleeding. Steve's mother and sisters had returned home within moments after his dad had hit his head. They just picked Dad up and carried him off to the bedroom. No one spoke to anyone else. Steve said again he thought, "Maybe this is all in my head." I asked the two older sisters and Steve's mother why they had not talked about this incident with Steve. They responded, "Because he hadn't said anything, and we hoped he hadn't noticed." Helplessness, despair, and

hopelessness cause family members to believe if you just ignore it, it may not hurt; if you just ignore it, it may just go away.

Fear and control often fuel the Don't Talk rule. Skip described his father as abstinent but without recovery. He controlled himself by not drinking and controlled his family with silence. "My dad didn't talk to me at all and my mother wouldn't acknowledge that there was anything wrong. My life was filled with this engulfing terribleness and I thought it was me. I wanted my father to tell me there was something wrong. I wanted him to tell me it was his fault. I wanted to hear it was not my fault. Later, as I got older, I needed him to tell me he was proud of me. I didn't get any of those things. I only got his silent rage." Skip's answer to this was to "keep a lid on" his feelings and his emotional self. Keeping the lid on fueled a major eating disorder. By fifth grade Skip weighed 250 pounds, and he would ultimately weigh 400 pounds. It was only when his father died that Skip would begin to shed his weight. With the need for emotional control over, the behavioral manifestation of his powerlessness no longer gripped Skip and his recovery would begin.

Many adult children have told me that they were instructed not to talk about things that would upset Mom or Dad; or they simply learned by themselves that things went much easier when they did nothing to "rock the boat." Andrew said, "Dinner was pretty quiet. Anything we said rocked the boat. And then, if we were too quiet, that rocked the boat!" These children not only don't talk about boat-rocking issues, but they don't talk about, or share, their fears, worries, or hurts with anyone.

In many families, the rule of silence is a quiet collusion. Children will share the same bedroom with a sibling for years, both hearing the arguing taking place between Mom and Dad. Or, they hear Mom crying night after night. But they only hear. They never speak to one another about it, although they may each cry—silently and alone. In one family, the six children were between the ages of twelve and twenty-one when Dad sought treatment for his addiction. Three to four months prior to seeking help, the father would return home late at night after having been drinking for several hours. Not having seen his children all day, he'd make his nightly rounds, passing from one room to another, until he'd seen each of his children. He would scream, shout, and harass each child before moving on to the next room. All of the children were awake as he went from room to room but they never spoke to each other about these nightly episodes. The family simply acted as though nothing out of the ordinary was happening.

Well-adjusted children who experience daily childhood problems would, most likely, talk about these things with other family members. In another family, young Billy told me how he was taking the air out of the car tires so Dad wouldn't drive when he was drinking. His youngest sister, Ann, was putting water in Dad's vodka bottle; his oldest sister, Lisa, was putting apple cider in Dad's whiskey. Each was unaware of the other's actions concerning Dad's drinking because they were unable to talk about the real issue—their father's substance abuse.

Because of the denial, seldom are any of these children's problems recognized. Moreover, the family problem—addiction—is never discussed. These children (accurately or inaccurately) do not perceive others, inside or outside of the family, to be available to them for help. Many adult children have questioned where their aunts and uncles were when they needed them. Many wondered why grandparents weren't more concerned for them.

Nora, another adult child, told me no one would have believed what her home life was like. "They wouldn't believe me, because if it was so bad, I couldn't be looking so good. They never saw my mother getting drunk every day; they never saw her raving like a maniac, passed out upstairs. They never saw her bottles all over the house. They just never saw."

While many children fear not being believed, they may also feel guilty. They believe they are betraying their parents and their family if they talk honestly. Children feel very loyal to their parents and, invariably, end up defending them, rationalizing that it isn't really all that bad and continuing in what has now become a denial process. Finding the family situation so confusing, they feel inadequate in attempting to verbalize the problems—they just don't know how to tell others. This makes it very easy to succumb to a sense of hopelessness or helplessness.

"As the alcoholism in my family progressed, the family got more and more silent and the house got more and more silent. We withdrew from each other. It got to the point we didn't talk to each other about much of anything. We couldn't even talk about 'safe' things, such as a television program. How could we ever talk about the things we knew weren't safe?"

It is as if they are wearing a pair of eyeglasses with clouded lenses from which to view the world. Perceptions are altered, their reality distorted. They continue to discount and minimize; they learn to tolerate inappropriate behavior. They learn to live in denial. It is most despairing to be a child in an addictive family, to feel totally alone, and to believe talking to someone will not help.

"Sometimes I pretend my mom is not drinking when she really is. I never even talk about it."

—Melody, age 9

Don't Trust

"I am always on my guard with people. I want to trust them, but it is so much easier to just rely on myself. I'm never sure what other people want."

Children raised in addictive families learn that it is not safe to trust others with the real issues in their lives. To trust another means investing confidence, reliance, and faith in that person. Confidence, reliance, and faithfulness are virtues often missing in the addictive home. Children need to be able to depend on parents to meet their physical and emotional needs in order to develop trust. Parents are not consistently available to their children because they are under the influence of alcohol or drugs, physically absent, mentally and emotionally consumed with their addiction, or preoccupied with the addicted person.

Joan can't count on her mom to be attentive about what she has to say after coming home from school. Joan's mom doesn't smile after hearing about something funny, nor is she very sensitive to Joan's sadnesses. Usually, Joan's mom is preoccupied with what happened or didn't happen last night as the result of Dad's drinking.

Carl doesn't trust people to see his feelings as important. He may be angry about something that happened on the way home from school, but he usually doesn't say anything about it because, "There's enough to be angry about at home. Who needs more? Besides, they wouldn't understand."

Dan cannot trust the decisions his parents make. He can't rely on his dad to remember a promise to go to a ball game on the weekend or the permission he gave Dan to spend a night at a friend's house. Nor can Dan count on his mom to support him if Dad goes back on his word.

Karen cannot rely on her mom to be sober for her birthday, Thanksgiving, or Christmas. While Karen cannot rely on her mom for sobriety during special occasions, Jason knows his mother will drink on those holidays. He said the uncertainty, the never knowing for sure how his stepfather was going to handle Mom's drunkenness was most confusing for him.

Allen, age thirty-two, described an incident when he was eleven years old. He had returned home from school and found his mother intoxicated. As he came through the door, she started an argument with him. She began to scream and shout at him and he began to scream and shout back. This was a typical after-school scene, but this time Mom picked up a broom and began hitting him about the head and shoulders. While Mom was screaming and hitting, Allen was ducking and hollering back at her. He ran to the telephone and called his father. (Allen's parents were divorced.) Allen was surprised when his father answered, but he did at least answer! Imagine the scene of eleven-year-old Allen yelling into the phone explaining what was happening, ducking the broom, while his mom screamed at him and continued hitting him. His father shouted back into the receiver, "Don't worry, she won't remember it tomorrow."

Twenty-one years later, when Allen related this incident to me, he spoke with no affect or expression in his voice. I responded, saying, "Allen, does that sound like a normal response to you?" Allen looked at me quizzically and said slowly, "Normal? I don't know. I guess I have never really thought about it." Of course Allen had not thought about it. Allen could not rely on his mother to be there, to respond appropriately to him emotionally, psychologically, physically, or to meet his needs in any way when he was an eleven-year-old boy. Allen could not rely on his father to understand his needs either, let alone offer protection while he was being physically abused. Allen wouldn't find it emotionally safe to allow himself to respond with hurt, anger, or disgust to his mother's beating or his father's lack of concern. But Allen did find it safe to detach himself and not to think about the incident. Allen, like so many others with similar experiences, learned not to trust.

In order for children to trust, they must feel safe. They need to be able to depend on their parents for friendly help, concern, and guidance in response to their physical and emotional needs. In addictive homes, however, children often cannot rely on parents to provide safety.

Debra tells how she never feels safe bringing friends home because, "It is always possible Mom will be drunk and do something to embarrass me." Scott said, "It is never safe to play in our yard because Dad always seems to be sure to belittle me when my friends are around." These children live in a fearful environment. For some, their lack of safety is more psychological; for others, it is psychological and physical. Children often tell of frightening times with a parent when he is driving recklessly or when fires are caused due to drunken neglect. Children's physical safety is directly threatened when verbal harassment turns violent, when furniture is being broken, or certainly when persons in the home are physically and/or sexually assaulted.

It is difficult to trust a person who constantly embarrasses, humiliates, disappoints, or puts you in physical jeopardy. It is even more difficult to trust when family members minimize, rationalize, and/or blatantly deny certain events are taking place.

Part of feeling safe is feeling security. This security is seldom present for any length of time in addictive homes. Tim comes home from school one day to discover his dad has lost his job for the fourth time in three years. It means the family will be moving again. For Tim, it means giving up some newfound friends at a school that was just beginning to become familiar to him. And it means giving up the opportunity to make more friends through Little League, which he just joined—another disappointment. Tammy finds out her dad gave away her purebred pet rabbits to a drinking buddy. She had been raising them from bunnies with the intention of entering them in the county fair—another hope shattered. David learns the family's long-planned summer vacation has to be canceled because Dad loaned the vacation money to a stranger he met at a local bar—another promise broken. Children are continually confronted with reasons to be insecure in their surroundings, to not trust.

Joe described his inability to trust this way. "Trust? My dad couldn't ever seem to take care of himself wherever he was. There was always a problem—at home, at work, with the car, with grandparents, with friends. If he couldn't take care of himself, how was he going to take care of me? No, I couldn't trust him for anything. And my mom, she was there, but that's all I can say. She was physically there, but I don't remember her ever trying to help us cope or understand. She was simply there."

Children constantly hear mixed messages, which teach distrust. A parent often gives a child false information intentionally in a feeble effort to protect the child from reality. A mother may tell the children she is happy when she is actually miserable. A father may reassure a child that nothing is wrong when the child can see mother is acting strangely. The child is confused because one message is coming from his parent's words and a contradictory message from the body movement and tone of voice. Such confusing messages propel the child into a life of second-guessing what is really happening.

The single, most important ingredient in a nurturing relationship is honesty. No child can trust, or be expected to trust, unless those around him are also open and honest about their own feelings. Addicted people lose their ability to be honest as the disease progresses. As the addict continues to drink or use, he has to rationalize his negative action and do it extremely well in order to continue his behavior. An addict's life is consumed with feelings of guilt, shame, anxiety, and remorse, causing him to drink or use all the more in an attempt to escape. It becomes a never-ending cycle because of the psychological and physical addiction. Enabling parents are fearful of being honest with their children. They don't want them to experience the same pain they are feeling. Moreover, they don't want to acknowledge that the problem exists in the first place.

While children don't require verbalization of all the feelings their parents' experience, they do need validation and/or clarification of certain specific situations and feelings. This validation or clarification doesn't happen in a home where *talking* and *trusting* do not exist.

A person takes a risk when he reaches out to trust another. Those persons who have learned to take the risk have experienced trusting to be a good process. They have also experienced a sense of security and a feeling of self-worth, both derived from feeling loved. All young people need to feel valued, to feel they are precious and special. While parents may tell them they are special and loved, it is the parents' behavior that allows a child to believe it.

Children need focused attention. Focused attention represents not only physically being with a child, but also interacting with the child in a way that says, "You have all of my attention—mentally and emotionally." Focused attention says to a child, "I care. It's important for me to be with you." Children are highly sensitive to the degree of focused attention they receive. A child receives no sense of value from parents who are forever absorbed in their own affairs. While children don't need exclusive attention, it is a lack of focused attention—when others never have time to truly be with them—that causes them to feel unimportant. As a parent's addiction progresses, it fuels isolation that makes him less available to his children. As well, the coaddict becomes increasingly preoccupied with both the addict and her own helplessness and hopelessness, decreasing her availability as a resource for the children.

Although these children are not totally ignored, as the addiction progresses the availability of focused time decreases. When these families do spend time together, that time is often centered on the addictive behavior. Tim, age fifteen, told how he was spending "special time" with his father. Both liked to fish and did so quite often during the summer. Although Tim always looked forward to the two of them spending time alone together, he was almost always disappointed because his father normally brought along a drinking buddy. Dad and his buddy got so involved in their drinking and carrying on that Tim might as well have been totally alone. Tim spent time with his dad, but the time spent did not allow Tim that "special time" meant just for him and his father. The father's attention was always focused elsewhere—with or without Tim around.

Children need focused attention most when they are under stress. Unfortunately, in an addictive family this is when they are least apt to receive it. Stress often becomes the norm in this environment and the attention centers around the addict. Thus, instead of turning attention to the child who may be having a problem, attention is turned away from the child, and the child's problem is never addressed.

Children often find they do not trust caring acts and are confused or suspicious of focused attention when it occurs. Because of broken promises and not being able to rely on the consistency of positive interaction, children are often confused. Such actions make the children not trust the motivation behind true focused attention.

A child may enjoy a day at the zoo but will question the motivation behind the trip. Although both parents may have agreed on the excursion, the child perceives only the addict's sense of guilt or the coaddict's dominance over the situation. Or, the child thinks maybe the parents do care in this one instance, but that feeling is overshadowed by the knowledge that neither parent may be relied on to be available at another important time in his or her life. They may always wonder, "Did Dad bring me this present because he didn't come to my piano recital last night, or because he saw it and wanted me to have it out of his love for me?"

While children can and do survive, problems arise in their lives because their environmental circumstances have made it impossible for them to feel safe and secure or to rely on or trust others. Trust is one of those vital character-building blocks children need in order to develop into healthy adults. Being raised in an addictive family structure often denies or distorts this portion of a child's development.

"I have a hard time trusting my mom."

—Chuck, age 6

Don't Feel

"No, I wasn't embarrassed. I was scared for my father, but I wasn't scared for myself. It didn't dawn on me to be scared for me. I wasn't disappointed.

> *I didn't really think about it. I never got angry with him. There was nothing to get angry about. I didn't cry much. What was there to cry about?"*

The above quotation says, "No, I don't feel. And if I do, it is a feeling for someone else. I can feel scared for my father or my sister but not for myself." As nine-year-old Chris said to me, "One time my dad got upset when he was drinking and he slapped me. I looked at my mom and she started crying. So I cried. I wasn't crying for me, I was crying for my mom." It has been my experience that by the time a child being raised in an addictive family reaches the age of nine, he has a well-developed denial system about his feelings and his perceptions of what is happening in the home.

Children do whatever they possibly can to bring stability and consistency into their lives. They will behave in any manner if it makes it easier for them to cope and survive. The role adoption described earlier assists children in coping with the inconsistencies in their lives. Learning to focus on the environment, or on other people, or learning to detach oneself from the family, assists children in not feeling.

The family law Don't Talk and the premise Don't Trust teach children that it isn't safe to share feelings. Children learn not to share and, inevitably, deny their feelings. They don't think family members, other relatives, or friends will validate their feelings. They don't believe their feelings will receive the necessary nurturing. Children don't perceive others as resources; therefore, they live their lives emotionally isolated. Being alone with feelings of fear, worry, embarrassment, guilt, anger, loneliness, etc., leads to a state of desperation or being overwhelmed. Such a state of being does not lend itself to survival, so the children learn other ways to cope. Some learn how to discount and repress feelings, while others learn simply not to feel. These children do have access to their feelings, but only with the help of a trusted person. For the majority of children growing up with addiction, however, trust and trusted persons are not a consistent part of their lives.

Denise is a cheerleader for her high school's basketball team. One evening, at an out-of-town game, her father arrives noticeably drunk. After having spent much of the evening yelling out to Denise during her routines, her father, who by this time is unable to walk himself out of the gym, drapes himself over the top of Denise, relying on her to get him out of the gymnasium and to the car. As she is slowly moving the two of them out of the gymnasium, he begins to yell and jeer at several students just behind them. His remarks are crude and vulgar and then he begins to scream racial slurs. With determination, Denise pushes her way through the crowd, holding her father tight to her. Behind her she hears the escalating remarks of the crowd. Suddenly they are outside. She races him to a car driven by one of his friends, leaves him, and then quietly makes her way to the pep bus.

Embarrassment, humiliation, fear, and anger are the common emotions a child in this situation would experience. But for Denise none of these emotions are conducive to her perception of how to handle the problem. Instead, the reaction of this most responsible eldest child is to take care of the situation and to get her father out of the gymnasium before he gets hurt.

Denise has learned if she lets feelings take over when an incident like the one just described occurs, it will only result in pain for herself. It doesn't occur to her to talk to anyone (a chaperone on the trip, a school friend) about the incident because she believes no one would really understand or, worse yet, that they would make unkind judgments about her and her father.

Only a few tears fell that night as Denise headed home. None of her schoolmates mentioned the incident and she most certainly didn't tell her mother about it. She knew that to discuss the incident would only bring more pain to the family. Denise has found it's a lot "safer" to ignore her feelings. For her, the feelings are too confusing, too complicated, and very scary. She hasn't found anyone she can trust to share those scared feelings with.

Any young person would feel disappointed if his parent didn't show up for at least one school event in the entire school year. A child from a healthy family would not only be disappointed, but angry as well. But for the child of a chemically dependent parent, this is just another one of those events to try not to feel bad about. It is easier not to feel anything than to dwell on the pain or the unfairness of it. And if the child does feel, it is easier to be angry with the nonaddicted parent when he or she misses an activity or to take the anger out on a classmate.

Again, it would be normal for Jerry to be disappointed, afraid, and angry when, as a child, he has been sent to stay with a relative because Mom's drinking became worse. When he returns in a couple of weeks, he's told Mom won't be drinking. But Jerry finds his mother exactly the way she was when he left home—drunk. The six-year-old in this situation might tell Dad he is angry (he hasn't yet learned to deny), but Jerry at age nine would just ignore it. He simply no longer allows himself to respond emotionally.

Love is caring enough to Help But Sometimes it runs out.

In these incidents of denial, the children are building up walls of self-protection. They are learning unhealthy coping mechanisms to protect themselves from the fear of their reality. The reality is that their parents are failing them. As the addiction progresses, the substance becomes the parents' obsession. When family members experience the results of this obsession, they ask the questions, "Why?" "Why does my mom disappoint me at important times?" "Why does my dad embarrass me like that?" "Doesn't he love me?" "Why is my dad drinking so much?" "Are my parents ever going to get better?" "Is she crazy?" "Is it my fault?" "Am I crazy?" It is frightening for family members to ask such questions of themselves. It can be even more frightening to allow themselves to honestly answer.

There is so much to feel about,
to be emotional about:

Afraid . . .
when Mom and Dad fight
to ask Mom when Dad will be coming home
to find out he may not be coming home
to tell Mom "No" about anything, for fear she'll get drunk and leave
of being in the car with Mom when she is driving while intoxicated
of getting hit when Dad is drunk and violent

Sad . . .
because we don't have any money, Dad can never keep a job
when I see my mother crying
when I have to sit in the car for hours and hours when Dad is in the bar
because my dad would rather be away than at home

Angry . . .
at Dad, for making excuses for my mom when she is just drunk
at others, for calling my mom a drunk
at Dad, for making promises and always breaking them
at Dad, for always being so critical

Embarrassed . . .
when Mom attended the school open house intoxicated
because Dad has passed out in the front yard
because Mom looks so sloppy half-dressed
when my dad tries to act sober but he isn't

Guilty . . .
thinking if I hadn't talked back to my mother this morning, she might not have gotten drunk
for never being able to do enough to please my dad
for hating someone I am supposed to love, my mom
for being ashamed of my parents for "being alive"

These are only a few of the multitude of feelings family members may experience on a daily basis—yet learn not to express. As a result, these persons often learn to discount and inevitably deny those feelings entirely. The reason for denying is to convince themselves, as well as others, that their unhappy family life can be made happy by pretending, or denying reality. People tend to deny and minimize both situations and feelings in order to hide their own pain. They don't want to be uncomfortable. The greatest problem here is that when someone minimizes and discounts feelings for not just weeks, but months and years of their life, it becomes a skill they take with them into adulthood that will permeate every significant area of their life.

Don't Talk, Don't Trust, and Don't Feel are the three major rules in the troubled family system. Yet other rules are also often experienced.

"The rules were: Don't question. Don't ask if you can get away with it. When you wanted attention and didn't get it, that was just the way it was. If they said you were going somewhere and you didn't, you had to accept it. If they said pick a bag of weeds for no good reason, you went and picked the bag of weeds. If they hit you, you did nothing, and you felt nothing."

Don't Think

Many children learn that it is not okay to think about what is happening. When it is not safe to talk or feel, it simply becomes easier not to think about what you are witnessing or experiencing.

Jessica told me, "We were taught not to think, not to speak, and not to feel. There were all of these kids in the same house, and it was as if there was this conspiracy among us. We were each other's witnesses, but it was as if our eyes and ears were closed. That was our form of self-protection. We silently accepted our doom. My mother, who was our model, was a quiet, religious woman. She was physically present when the abuse was going on, but she never spoke of it and somehow shut her ears to it."

Don't Question

The rules Don't Think and Don't Question go hand in hand. "When Mom doesn't come home, don't question. When Dad contradicts himself mid-sentence, don't question. When plans are canceled, don't question. It's just easier that way."

Don't Ask

Don't Ask means more than don't ask questions. It means don't initiate asking for anything. Don't ask for more information—you may be ridiculed or shamed. Don't ask for something you want or need—you know you will be denied. You either learn not to ask or, as in Jason's case, nearly have an anxiety attack when doing so.

Jason, who is eleven, needs twenty dollars to play in the band at school for a special event. He waits for his parents to come home. He knows they will be loaded; there is never a good time to ask for anything. He has rehearsed his request for hours. He has several times talked himself out of the need for the money to play in the band. He literally finds himself shaking as his parents enter the house. As they come through the door, his father sees him and quickly yells, "What are you still doing up at midnight, Punk? You ought to be in bed." Jason responds, "I've got to talk to you. I need some money for a pair of black pants so I can march with the band." Dad responds, "A marching band? Does that school think we're a money tree? Tell your teacher to come over here and tell me to my face that I've got to foot the bill for some pansy band uniform. I'll tell him a thing or two." Jason's mom yells at her husband to shut up, and the focus shifts, both parents now arguing with each other, forgetting about Jason and his request.

After a few experiences such as that, you not only learn not to ask; you learn not to expect. Jason is not angry or even disappointed with his parents. He is angry with himself for being hopeful.

Don't Play

Many children learn it is not safe to play. "Who will take care of my little sister if I am outside?" "I can't take time to play. I need to stay with the adults to know what is going to happen next." For some, it is too painful to go play with others when their thoughts and feelings are focused on what is happening at home. It is easier to just stay at home—watch and be vigilant. Others find that their only validation comes when they are being "mature."

They are not supported and cherished for being who they are, but only acknowledged and validated for being a premature adult.

Don't Make a Mistake

Many learn mistakes will not be tolerated. Jerry, age thirty-four, can remember his first mistake. "I was six. It was my first and my last mistake. I was eating a bowl of cereal with my dad and I spilled the milk. He backhanded me. I flew off the stool, hit my head up against the refrigerator door, and had a headache for the next three days. I have never made another mistake."

The dysfunctional family rules are a way of life in addictive families. Children learn how to live without the truth being told. They learn to keep their mouths shut and pretend problems do not exist. Denial of what is going on in the home creates a severe distortion of perception. Children learn not to see the world clearly. As they move into adulthood, they find themselves wearing a distorted pair of glasses with which they view the world. They continue to discount, minimize, and tolerate inappropriate behavior by not questioning. As part of this process, they develop a painful, high tolerance for inappropriate behavior. When the three basic rules, Don't Talk, Don't Trust, Don't Feel, are combined with the other dysfunctional rules, it is easy to see how a child easily becomes dispirited and moves into a coping role.

"John, why do you think other people feel angry, scared, and disappointed, but you don't?"

"Maybe because I have to be tough!"

—John, age 13

Chapter 4

Progression of the Roles

Children raised in addictive homes enter adulthood coping with life's problems in ways that have proved to be of great value to them. These include being responsible, adjusting, or placating, as well as not talking, not feeling, and not trusting. Reaching young adulthood, adult children go on about their lives continuing to applaud themselves for being survivors. As adults, however, they find no reason to change these patterns, which have always ensured survival.

The Responsible Child

The oldest or only child, the one who became the little adult, continues into the grown-up world carrying a lot of responsibility. The ability to be responsible has been a great strength in that this young adult has already demonstrated maturity in handling many different kinds of situations. He or she continues to take charge and often assumes leadership roles. As a child, this person learned to set realistic goals during very early years, and as a young adult, he or she has realized a number of accomplishments far sooner than most people. But, there also has been an evolution. This adult person now becomes tense, experiences increased anxiety, and often feels separated from others by an invisible wall.

During their adolescent years, children who adopted the responsible role were so busy being young adults that there was no time to be children. They didn't have time to relax as children, and as a consequence, they don't know how to relax as adults. These children have been taking life so seriously for so many years that now, in adulthood, they are awkward and uncomfortable and have a very difficult time joining in fun.

"I still try to take a lot of responsibility for people and things. I am only beginning to learn how to play. I find it difficult to enjoy hobbies or fun activities with any great consistency."

Chris, who had so organized and structured her own childhood, became a very rigid person, lacking in flexibility. As a child, she needed to be in charge, or at least feel she was in control. If not, she had a sense that her entire world was collapsing. As an adult, this phenomenon continues. Chris finds herself needing to take charge, to feel in absolute control. If not, there is a pervasive sense of losing control and being totally overwhelmed.

"The idea of loss of control is intolerable to me. I get panicky when I try to think of it."

Joe has to be in charge. Joe tries to fit himself in structured positions and, ideally for him, positions he is able to control. He has to be in the one-up position, while someone else always has to be in the one-down position. There is no room in his life for an equal relationship. That would ultimately mean giving up control, which, for Joe, would be giving up survival.

One-up, one-down, and win-lose relationships are common in many professional, social, and intimate relationships. Remember, those responsible youngsters have become rigid, serious, goal-attaining young adults who have confidence in their ability to accomplish a great deal. No sense of equal relationships exists for these persons, nor does a sense of problem solving. These adults speak well (a skill learned as youngsters) and have mastered the ability to mask the reality of their earlier family life. For these responsible adult children everything is all or nothing, one way or the other. There is no in-between.

Jenna is an only child of an alcoholic father. At the age of thirty-one, she had become a lawyer in private practice, an apparent success. Unfortunately, she was alone in that private practice because two attempts at working with other professionals had failed. She lacked close female friends, and her third attempt at marriage was failing. Jenna had developed those traits similar to so many other children raised with addiction. She had not learned to trust that other people would be available when they were needed. As with many children of addiction, she also found it easier to rely on herself, not involving others. Jenna is outwardly successful, yet inwardly, someone who cannot bring herself to trust that others will be there for her. She can't depend on others and therefore has no recourse but to relate on an unequal basis. She doesn't know how to have fun, nor can she talk about the real issues for herself, and she certainly can't talk about her feelings. In her personal and professional relationships, this responsible person is almost forced to associate with others who are equally emotionally inaccessible. Should she find a very feeling, articulate, open, caring, fun-loving person in her life, she would not know how to respond.

A sharing, intimate relationship would be too uncomfortable so the adult child removes herself or himself from that type of relationship. In fact, responsible children often align themselves with people who allow them to continue to be rigid, serious and unfeeling. Either that, or they separate themselves from others completely and continue to pursue very isolated lifestyles. It is easy to see why so many responsible children, who are now young adults, find themselves depressed, lonely, anxious, tense, and fearful. It is also easy to see how and why they often enter into unhealthy personal relationships.

The Responsible Child

Strengths	Deficits
• Organized	• Inability to listen
• Leadership skills	• Inability to follow
• Decision maker	• Inability to play
• Initiator	• Inability to relax
• Perfectionist	• Inflexibility
• Goal oriented	• Need to be right
• Self-discipline	• Severe need to be in control
	• Extreme fear of mistakes
	• Lack of spontaneity

Beliefs that Drive Behavior of Responsible Child

"If I don't do this, no one will."
"If I don't do this, something bad will happen or things will get worse."

Response to Feelings

"I must stay in control of my feelings."

"I was the all-American kid. In high school, I maintained a 3.6 grade point average and was a star on the championship baseball team. I was always trying to please my parents. Dad was alcoholic and a compulsive gambler. Mom worked seven days a week to support the family. After high school, I went into business for myself, but something was wrong. I was empty inside and didn't know why. Whatever I did just wasn't good enough. The more I achieved, the worse I felt. The accomplishments didn't mean anything. I couldn't fill the emptiness—it was always there. Finally, I couldn't face life anymore and had to turn to drugs and alcohol."

The Adjuster

Children who found it so much easier to shrug their shoulders and withdraw upstairs to the bedroom or slip out to a friend's house usually continue these survival patterns into their grown-up years. Adult adjusters find it easier to avoid situations where they need to take control. They function better if they

take whatever occurs in stride. They have become adept at adjusting, being flexible and spontaneous. They find pride in these traits. As Jason said, "I went to nine different schools as a kid. I never knew how long I would stay or where I was going next. It wasn't bad. I learned how to make friends quickly. I met a lot of interesting people." Now, as an adult, Jason still finds it necessary to keep moving. "I get bored in one spot. I get bored if I am at a job more than nine months. I get bored with the same woman after nine months. I am even getting bored with this city. I have been here two years now."

Children who adopt the adjusting pattern find they have neither the opportunity to develop trust on an ongoing basis, nor the ability to develop healthy relationships.

Jeff, who was raised in an abusing, alcoholic family, said, "More than anything, I was scared. I didn't have lots of friends, but I didn't want lots of friends. I did have two friends growing up. I think they came from homes like mine. I don't know really—we never talked. We hung around the playgrounds a lot. When I had to be home, I watched television if I could. If someone wanted to change the channel I let them. I just tried to be quiet. I liked to draw a lot so I did that. I never showed my drawings to anyone. They would have made fun of me."

All their lives, they seem to be jumping in, in the middle. It is difficult to identify a beginning or see the end. Adjusters, who as children never knew how long they would be living in one place, or how long Mom would be sober, or how long Dad would be staying away, learned how to handle (or adjust to) whatever situation they were currently in.

> *"I usually had a movie playing in my head. I was always the star, the heroine—strong and powerful and beautiful. I also had an imaginary friend who provided constant companionship and comfort. Fantasizing was my only protection from living continually in pain."*

Adjusters often have neither a sense of direction, nor a sense of taking responsibility for the direction they would like to take their lives. They feel no sense of choice or power over their own lives. While the more responsible children have developed a sense of being able to affect the events in their lives, adjusters usually do not have a sense of control. As forty-four-year-old Janice said, "I feel like I have been on a roller coaster for a real long time."

For adjusting children, life is a perpetual roller coaster—not because they like living that way, but because they feel they have no other options. They perceive themselves as having no alternatives. They never learned that choices were available to them. So now, as adults, they don't talk about real issues in their lives, and they certainly do not seriously examine their own feelings. Adjusters find themselves associating with others who are as emotionally closed as they are. This limited association is the only type of relationship they find safe.

Based on this behavior pattern, it is easy to see how adjusters find mates who cause uproar. This state of living in constant agitation becomes their comfort zone because they are perpetuating childhood roles of adapting to inconsistent people. They know how to handle chaotic situations—adjust. This kind of self-negating adjusting leads to depression, isolation, and loneliness.

The Adjuster

STRENGTHS	DEFICITS
• Flexibility	• Inability to initiate
• Ability to follow	• Fear of making decisions
• Easy going attitude	• Lack of direction
• Not upset by negative situations	• Inability to perceive options, power
	• Follows without questioning

Beliefs that Drive Behavior of Adjuster

"If I don't get emotionally involved, I won't get hurt."
"I can't make a difference anyway."
"It is best not to draw attention to myself."

Response to Feelings

"Why should I feel? It's better if I don't."

The Placater

The child who was busy taking care of everyone else's emotional needs—the warm, sensitive, caring, listening child, the one everyone liked—grows up continuing to take care of others, either personally or occupationally. As a very special friend of mine once said, "Those of us in the helping professions did not gravitate here accidentally. There must have been something wrong with us to be so preoccupied day in and day out with the pain of others." Though this statement was said in half jest, it carries an enormous amount of truth. For the child who was particularly adept at making others feel comfortable, it's only natural to gravitate toward situations that would enable him or her to continue in that manner.

> *"There is something about me that seems to attract sick individuals or simply people with some type of problem."*

Forty-four-year-old Elaine was raised in a home by two alcoholic parents. When one takes care of others over the years, it is not unusual to arrive at the point Elaine eventually reached. She proceeded to enter into marriages with three different practicing alcoholics. When her third husband was hospitalized for his alcoholism, I asked her during a private session, "While your husband is in this program, what can you do for you so you'll feel better?" Elaine looked away. She began to grimace. She didn't answer my question, nor did she look at me. So I repeated the question. "Elaine, while your husband is in the hospital for the next three weeks, what can you do for you so you'll feel better?" Again Elaine looked away, but this time in addition to making grimacing gestures with her face, her shoulders began to twitch and jerk. The jerking was almost spasmodic.

Reaching out to steady her, I said, "Elaine, you don't have to take care of your husband anymore! You don't have to take care of him! We are going to take care of him. And you don't have to take care of your two boys tonight. You've already told me they are with friends. It is seven o'clock now. Between seven o'clock and ten o'clock tonight, what are you going to do for you so you will feel better?" There was a pause but no grimacing, no jerking. Elaine simply said the only thing she could have said.

With tears running down her cheeks, she whispered, "I don't know, I don't know."

Of course she didn't know. All her life, the question of what she could do for herself was not a question she could safely explore. Adults who grew up in the role of placaters typically go through years of adulthood never seriously considering what they want. Instead, they discount their needs. They have trained themselves only to be concerned with providing for others, consequently never getting what they want from life. For the placater, survival was taking away the fears, sadnesses, and guilts of others. Survival was giving of one's time, energy, and empathy to others. Surviving had nothing to do with their personal needs. And as Diane, a forty-eight-year-old woman married to a recovering alcoholic, said, "I am that compulsive giver. I need to become more selfish. I must quit serving everyone else at my own expense, but I don't know how. I feel so guilty." Giving to others is not bad, but giving at the expense of our own well-being is destructive.

Again, it is relatively easy to understand why these children develop depression as adults. Although they appear to be living their lives the way they want, they still feel apart from others; they feel lonely. They don't have equal relationships with others. They always give too much and refrain from putting themselves in a position to receive. In personal relationships, placaters seek out people who are takers and who refuse to take emotional responsibility in themselves. They look for people who don't want personal sharing from a friend or loved one. As well, the placaters' partners in life will be people who have also learned not to talk about themselves.

The Placater

Strengths	Deficits
• Caring	• Inability to receive
• Empathetic	• Inability to focus on self
• Good listener	• Guilty
• Sensitive to others	• Strong fear of anger
• Gives well	• High tolerance for inappropriate behavior
• Nice smile	
• Warm	

Beliefs that Drive Behavior of Placater

"If I am nice, people will like me."
"If I focus on someone else, the focus won't be on me and that is good."
"If I take care of you, you won't leave me or reject me."

Response to Feelings

"I must take care of others' feelings."

She Was My Mother Bless Her Soul

I sometimes sit
in the corner
in the dark
and recall my mother
with a brown bottle in her hand
or the sounds of clanking ice at 2 a.m.
She'd call me baby if she wanted another beer
or a slut if she hadn't had enough.
She'd make me cookies on Christmas
before she'd get too drunk.
Many nights
she would fall asleep on the floor.
I'd cover her with a blanket
and put a pillow under her head.
I'd awaken in the morning
to the sounds of her
screaming.
She wasn't an easy woman to please.
Most of the time
we didn't get along.
Sometimes I miss her
and the loneliness.

—Jane

The Acting-Out Child

The acting-out children, the ones who were constantly in trouble and caused problems, will continue to find conflicts in early adulthood. As children and as adults, they do not know how to feel good about themselves. They have been unable to interact with others in acceptable ways and have been unable to express their own needs or have them met. They were always aware of their anger but seldom aware of any other feelings.

> *"I spent most of my years dominated with anger and resentment. I transferred my pain by fighting someone, anyone. I didn't care if I won or lost. I would fight with words. I would fight with my fists. I was blind to the consequences. Fighting was a way of releasing negative feelings dammed up inside. It gave me a way, at least for a moment, to feel I had some power over my life force. It was energy. It compensated for the nothingness."*

Children usually gravitate toward others with similar personality traits to form a peer group. Acting-out children seldom respond to positive role models, and they usually become socially isolated. If they had been institutionalized in youth, they most often continue this pattern in their adult years.

Whether addicted or not, upon reaching adulthood, acting-out children find their behavior (or lack of it) has caused major problems. This behavior now complicates their adult lives because they may lack a high school education, frequently challenge authority, cannot control their anger (causing the loss of jobs), possibly have illegitimate children or youthful marriages. It is also typical for the acting-out child to have many of the qualities of the adjuster. This combination leads to a feeling of an even greater sense of powerlessness in their lives. Yet these children have strengths often not tapped.

The Acting-Out Child

STRENGTHS
- Close to own feelings
- Less denial, greater honesty
- Creative

DEFICITS
- Inappropriate expressions of anger
- Inability to follow direction

- Sense of humor
- Ability to lead without questioning
- Intrusive
- Social problems at young ages (truancy, addiction, high school dropout, teen pregnancy, etc.)

Beliefs that Drive Behavior of Acting-Out Child

"If I scream enough, someone may notice me."
"Take what you want. No one is going to give you anything."

Response to Feelings

"I am angry about it, whatever it is."

Mixing and Matching

Some children may clearly fit into one or more of these four roles. For most though, there are both primary and secondary roles.

John described himself predominantly as the responsible one, but at times of violence in his home he moved into the adjusting role. Since he was young, he believed he needed to take the pressure off his mother. His father seldom worked and would spend his days away from home. Neither Mom nor the kids knew how Dad filled most of his time. John took it upon himself to take charge of keeping the house clean and seeing that his brother and sister were kept entertained while his mother worked ten to twelve hours a day. On a daily basis, it was John who created order in the home. After school he would walk to where his mother worked, get money to go to the grocery store, get dinner ready, clean up the house, and see that his brother and sister did their homework. He certainly experienced the stress but didn't understand it. Mom seemed to be accepting of the situation, as she didn't complain openly although she was very harried and appeared sad.

His father talked a lot about working, but John doesn't really remember his dad having any steady jobs. John was a good student, bringing pride to his father. He can remember listening to his father brag about him to his drinking buddies. Over the years his father's behavior at home became frightening as he was increasingly intoxicated. He frequently accused the children of liking their mother more than him. His paranoia was often sexual in nature—being suspicious of his wife, accusing her of sexual affairs, accusing his daughter of being sexual with boys (when she was only eleven years old). His inappropriate behavior would escalate and he would become verbally abusive, frequently lying, and ultimately become physically violent, often threatening to kill the whole family.

John described the incredible fear he felt as his father began to take siege in their home. John said there was no illusion of his power. All he knew at these times was it was best to lie low, become invisible. Do not draw any attention to himself, disappear into the woodwork if possible. At such times, it was everyone for themselves. Not because he wasn't concerned about his sister and mother, but to do anything was provocation to his father.

While those times lasted only from minutes to hours, it was the intensity experienced, not the duration, that created an impact. John would move from being the responsible child to the adjuster in a literal fight for survival. Decades later, at times when John would feel frightened, he would again depart from being a capable, responsible adult and feel as if he were twelve years old and responding to the terror of his father's threats all over again.

Sarah described herself as mostly acting-out, but within her group of peers she became a placater. At home she was blatantly angry and often sullen. She talked back to her mother and was verbally abusive to her sister. In junior high she was sneaking out of the house to be with friends. She performed poorly in school, not paying much attention and frequently skipping classes by high school. But when she was with her friends she wanted only to please them. She created and was a part of the conflict at home, but in her peer group she frequently did what she could to keep peace among her friends. It was with her friends that she had a greater sense of being a part of, of belonging. She didn't understand what was happening at home and did not feel valued. With her friends, however, there was a way for her to be accepted.

A percentage of children will change and adopt different roles as they grow older. They tend to do this as their environment changes and they find the old role no longer serves its purpose or a new role creates greater security. Erica would move from being the responsible/placater to acting-out as her initial roles simply no longer worked for her. She was helping to raise her three younger brothers. Her mother was loaded most of the time. After a while the responsibilities became too great and her efforts seemed futile. Her brothers were no longer obeying her. She started to stay away from home. When home, she was frustrated with the different men who kept coming in acting as if they were her "dad" and then taking charge of the family. Ultimately, she began to hang out on the streets. The placater disappeared, and the ability to take charge, to initiate and organize would redirect itself in her acting out and becoming a leader on the streets.

In the following situation Ronnie would find the need to shift roles to garner more stability in his life. Both of Ronnie's parents were addicts. His mother was addicted to pills and alcohol and his father was hooked on a combination of drugs and alcohol. He was the third child, with his two brothers being four and six years older than he. He always relied on his older brothers, and they took good care of him. He doesn't remember a lot about his early childhood but describes it mostly as seeing his brothers as his parents. They dressed him. They saw to it that he went to school. When he was in grade school he can remember one of them meeting him at school and walking him home every day for a couple of years. His father wasn't around much of the time. When his dad was home, he was mostly quiet and aloof. The older brothers also took care of their mother. He described the situation as one where it was as if Mom needed a parent to tell her what she had to do, such as getting dressed, eating, maybe signing papers for school, or seeing that certain bills were paid. If anything, Ronnie described himself as a placater, wanting to please his older brothers. When the two older brothers left the home, he was just thirteen. "There was no one there to take care of Mom and she was in no shape to take care of herself most of the time, so I took over that role. It was not so much that I was trying to please her, I just moved into the responsible parenting role to keep her alive and I guess a place for me to stay."

For some children, needing to shift roles seems more connected to their reactions to individuals than the general environment.

> *"By the time I was eleven I had begun to confront my parents and tried to act as a mediator in their fights. I became the caretaker, the people pleaser, and the scapegoat. I had to take on all of these roles because there was only one of me. I'd switch into whatever role I thought would solve the situation.*

I became everything to everyone. I could be the perfect child, I made good grades, I was popular, I ordered the groceries, did the dishes. I made both my parents laugh. I was needed! Still, I was never sure when I came home if I was the selfish brat or the adored child."

There are strengths and deficits with each role children adopt. Unfortunately, because the skills developed within the roles are often acquired from a basis of fear and shame, they become extreme ways of coping and reacting. These coping behaviors also fuel problems due to undeveloped skills. It is vital to know how to initiate, but if you do not learn how to follow, it creates problems when you need to relate to others. It is good to be flexible, but if you never learn to make an autonomous decision, you risk victimization or never having your needs met. It is important to stand up for your rights and own your anger, but if you cannot identify other feelings, you lose the opportunity for intimacy. Self-reliance is a wonderful virtue, but at the price of never trusting others, it creates painful isolation. The key to healing is in finding balance.

Fueling Addiction

It is not possible to discuss the passing down of addiction in a family without acknowledging the role of genetic predisposition. The latest brain chemistry research shows a biological basis for addiction and tolerance. Studies have also shown that addiction repeats itself within the family from generation to generation. A conservative estimate is that 60 percent of all substance abusers have, or have had, at least one addicted parent. Twin studies and studies of children of alcoholics adopted close to birth offer compelling evidence of a fourfold increased risk for severe alcohol problems. (See Suggested Reading in the appendix.) The discovery that alcoholism is influenced by biology doesn't mean genes alone cause severe alcohol problems. No one is predestined to become alcoholic, any more than anyone has 100 percent chance for developing cancer or heart disease. Environmental factors also play a serious role.

While it is common for children who recognize they are being raised with chemical dependency to say they will not drink or use when they get older, in reality, most of them choose to do so. They begin drinking and using at about the same ages and for the same reasons that children from nonaddicted families make similar choices. These youngsters usually begin to drink in their early teens. Like their peers, they drink to have fun, because their friends want them to, or out of curiosity and defiance. They drink to feel grown up—they drink to escape. Most teenagers typically drink just to get drunk. They are experimenting. But most significantly, they drink with an added belief—*it will never happen to me*. They may recognize their parent is chemically dependent but they believe that addiction is based on a lack of willpower, that it is a control issue. This belief says, "I have seen enough and I know enough about what alcohol and drugs can do to a person. I will be different."

For a child who has grown up with confusion, fear, shame, and powerlessness, alcohol and drugs offer more than what they offer young people from healthier families. While chemical dependency is the most likely addiction to pass generationally, it is also common that children, in an attempt to make sure they do not repeat the patterns of their parent(s), resort to a different substance or behavior to meet their needs. If it is not alcohol or drugs, it may be disorders with food, money, or sex for children affected by addiction in the family.

Responsible Child

For the responsible child, alcohol helps them loosen up and relax. When they drink, they aren't quite as serious. Although these same personality changes occur in most people who drink, for those who are stuck in unhealthy patterns, alcohol may be the only thing that provides relief. Taking a drink makes them feel adequate—a feeling which to be sustained leads from one drink to another and then another. When these individuals drink they are able to become more open with their feelings, show some vulnerability, and discover that other people respond to them more positively when they exhibit this relaxed and open manner. This does not necessarily make them chemically dependent, but it does reinforce their need to drink and sets them up for a psychological dependency.

> *"I was this perfect kid. Academically, I did well and got a lot of satisfaction from being a part of the 'in' group. I belonged. I had the right*

girlfriend. My family looked good to the outsiders. But by the time I went to college, I was emotionally numb, confused, but wasn't looking back. I had seen enough alcohol to float a small country. But excessive drinking made drinking seem normal to me. So when I began to have a drink every night before going to bed, it didn't strike me that no one else in the dorm had a drink every night, or took a bottle of vodka with them to classes, or put liquor in a mouthwash bottle. I drank to relax, to relieve pain, to hide from alienation and vague feelings of anxiety. But mostly to get rid of, to hide, or to mask the way I felt. It was also the time in which I felt closest to my dad."

Adjuster

For adjusters, alcohol removes feelings of inadequacy. Alcohol and other drugs can give them a false sense of power. Under the influence of alcohol and drugs they may find themselves aware of undiscovered options and alternatives. Making decisions becomes easier, as does experiencing honest feelings and talking about the real issues. With this newfound power comes increased self-confidence. But, in order to maintain these feelings it seems reasonable to have another drink, and another, and yet another. Ultimately, alcohol provides a "state of being" that feels good. It becomes a way of experiencing feelings, which can't seem to be experienced except with the use of alcohol. Again, it sets them up for a psychological dependency.

"I loved alcohol from the first swallow. I had been a time bomb waiting to explode. I had finally found a way to connect, to be a part of. It fixed me, something to make me feel adequate, okay, and able to cope."

Placater

Alcohol performs wonders for many placaters. Drinking helps them talk more freely about themselves, helping them to feel more self-worth. The drug, alcohol, helps placaters to become more assertive and to feel a greater selfishness. It empowers them to feel and even be angry. If alcohol provides feelings of increased self-worth, an avenue to become more selfish, a part of all placaters will respond positively to that feeling. In fact, they find they need that support to bolster such feelings. Ultimately, drinking becomes the problem solver. Like adjusters and responsible adult children, many placaters often have a second, a third, a fourth drink, or joint or toke. Before long, the psychological trap of dependency has become a reality.

> *"I wasn't a happy child. I was always trying to make sure I was liked. I tried so hard to please everyone. It was tiring. I remember being thirteen and at a girlfriend's house and a bunch of us were drinking screwdrivers. I was walking home and noticing that my lip was numb. I thought it felt wonderful and I wished that I could always feel that way. And then I started to smoke pot and thought this stuff is great for me. I saw the world in a whole different light. It wasn't long before I was using pot almost every day. I used it to maintain. Then I drank for total oblivion."*

Acting-Out Child

Alcohol and drugs are the typical trademarks of rebellious acts for many problematic children. Alcohol allows them to feel better about themselves. It gives them a false sense of confidence in their abilities. While most acting-out children experiment with alcohol and drugs, some quickly become abusers and develop their chemical dependency at earlier ages than other children from addictive families.

At age forty-six, Patty is still acting out her anger. She was an angry teenager and has been an angry adult. In spite of having a college degree, her addiction has blocked her career and she has resorted to supporting herself as a bartender. She has been married three times. She has relinquished the parenting of her children to the different fathers. Known for her belligerent attitude, she has challenged nearly everyone in authority positions, from her bosses to police. As a result, few people welcome her presence in their lives today.

> *"I began to use and drink when I was about twelve. I was so angry and was always in trouble, and in the beginning it calmed me down. It made it easier to get along with friends. I was already out of the house as much as I could be. It didn't take long until it seemed I just got into more trouble, but I didn't care. I had found something to fix me, something to fill up the horrible empty hole and at the same time make me feel able to cope."*

Joe summarized it all by saying, "I could play any role. I played them one right after another, never knowing who I was and never being me. I hated the insanity and the abuse in my family. Everything was out of control. The whole thing was nuts and I hated it—my mother's hysteria, my father's drinking. I wanted to kill myself, but never got the courage, so I let alcohol and drugs do it for me."

Chapter 5

Shame Circle

"The shame I feel over my own addiction is a refinement and purification of the shame I felt as a child over my father's alcoholism. On an emotional level, I drank a liquor twice brewed."

Shame is an accumulation of painful feelings that come with the belief that who we are is not good enough. We experience shame when we think of ourselves as inadequate, insufficient, or "less than." Other words descriptive of shame are to think of oneself as stupid, bad, ugly, dirty, damaged, or damaged goods.

When we pull away layers of shame we typically find abandonment. It may be both physical and emotional abandonment or it could be only emotional. In either situation, it is traumatic to children in their development.

Physical Abandonment

For some children, the abandonment is primarily physical. Physical abandonment occurs when the physical conditions necessary for thriving have been replaced by:

- Lack of appropriate supervision. *"We were left a lot with our older sister, but then she would leave too. We were mostly just three kids left alone. We tried not to be scared."*
- Inadequate provision of nutrition and meals; inadequate clothing, housing, heat, or shelter. *"We never had the basics. We never had enough underwear or socks. We never had slippers. There was a major sense of being without. No one told us how to keep clean, or how often. No one told us what to wear. One time the school called to have my sister picked up and taken home to have a bath. We kids tried so hard. We*

did our own laundry. We fixed our own food. We tried to keep things orderly but we had no space that was our own."

- Physical and/or sexual abuse. *"We never really knew what provoked them. They were quick to raise their voices or hit us. Mom would pick a fight with me out of nowhere and hit me. We could be doing something that we had done lots of times without them ever saying anything and then the next time we'd do it, they'd notice and we'd get hit for it. If you didn't do the dishes right, you could get hit. It never made sense."*

When caretakers don't provide safety in our environment, we grow up believing that the world is an unsafe place, that people are not to be trusted, and that we do not deserve positive attention and adequate care. This way of life becomes a legacy that we accept, not knowing how to make it different.

Emotional Abandonment

"Sometimes it seems as if I was abandoned emotionally. Other times it feels as if I was never claimed in the first place."

While children who experience physical abandonment will also endure emotional abandonment, it is more common to only experience the latter.

Two ways in which to understand emotional abandonment are:

1. Abandonment is experienced by parental indifference to a child's needs and wants, or the parents (or other primary caregivers) are emotionally unavailable on an ongoing basis. They do not offer the support and love a child needs.
2. Abandonment occurs when we have to hide a part of ourselves in order to be accepted or to avoid rejection. Those parts we learn to hide are:
   - Mistakes. For many children, to make a mistake, to be less than perfect, draws punitive responses.
   - Feelings. Being told the way you feel is not true or okay. "You have nothing to cry about and if you don't stop crying I will really give you something to cry about." "That really didn't hurt." "You have nothing to be angry about." This is not about

the occasional time a parent becomes frustrated with a child and makes such a comment, but a family situation where there is continual discounting of a child's emotions.

- Needs. Everyone else's needs appear to be more important than yours, and the only way you get attention is by attending to the needs of others.
- Successes. Accomplishments are not acknowledged, are many times discounted, or even used as ammunition to shame a child.

Other acts of abandonment occur when:

- We cannot live up to the expectations of our parents because such expectations are unrealistic and not age appropriate, such as expecting an eight-year-old to remember her dental appointment or the twelve-year-old to be able to manage his younger siblings for hours at a time.
- We are held responsible for other people's behavior and constantly blamed for the actions and feelings of parents or siblings.
- Disapproval is aimed at our entire being or identity rather than a particular behavior. This may involve being told that we are worthless when we have not done our homework or that we are never going to be a good athlete because we missed the final catch of the game. Our worth or value as a person is not separated out from our actions.

Abandonment and Boundaries

We experience abandonment when parents have a distorted sense of boundaries—their boundaries and ours. This happens when:

- Parents do not view us as separate beings with distinct boundaries.
- Parents expect us to be extensions of them, fulfilling their dreams.
- Parents are not willing to take responsibility for their feelings, thoughts, and behaviors but expect us to take responsibility for them.
- Parents' self-esteem is derived through our behavior, when their needs override ours.
- We are treated as peers with no parent/child distinction.

When this occurs at a time when children are developing their sense of worth, it is the foundation for the belief of their inadequacy, which is the core of toxic shame.

When parents are disrespectful of a child's boundaries and violate them, the message given is that they don't value the child as a person. That message becomes internalized as "I am not of value. I am not worthy." When parents don't acknowledge a child's boundaries, the message they give is "You are here to meet my needs" and/or "I am more important than you" and/or "It is not okay to be your own person with individual feelings, desires, or needs." The message also implies that the children have to give up themselves to be available to another person. This results in the internalized belief "I am bad for having different or separate needs, wants, and feelings." "I, in my uniqueness, am not of value." When we live with chronic abandonment due to distorted boundaries, we live in fear and doubt about our own worth.

Abandonment plus distorted or undefined boundaries as you are developing your worth and identity creates shame and fear.

Abandonment + Distorted/Undefined Boundaries
= Shame and Fear

Survival is about defending against our pain. The following are the many ways we defend and respond to our pain and mask our shame.

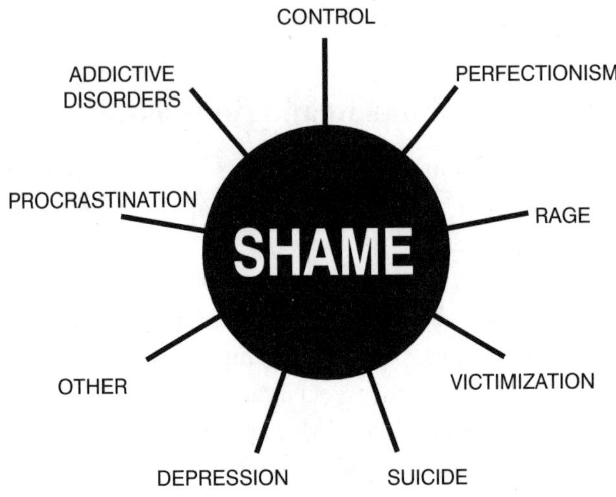

Control

Children learn to control in two ways, external and internal. The responsible child is often the master of external control, manipulating people, places, and things. This is the child who is the parent to brothers and sisters and to themselves. As Chris said, "I raised myself rather well." Tim set the bedtime for his younger brother and sister and made sure they had bathed and were tucked in. He made their lunches for school the next morning. Kimberly would call her father to tell him what he needed to do when he came home from work. All children are likely to try to control the internal, intangible aspect of their personal lives. They do that by withholding their feelings and diminishing their needs, neither expecting nor asking for anything.

"I am not angry. What is there to be angry about?"

"I wasn't embarrassed. I'm used to those things by now."

"I don't need to go to my friend's house. Who would be home to take care of my sister?"

"I don't want a birthday. Dad wouldn't show up anyway."

This is self-control, protection to ward off further pain by repressing desires and feelings. When we were children our attempt to control internally or externally was about survivorship. It made sense in the context of our environment.

Unfortunately, the continued need for control causes problems in our adult lives. We have spent years being hypervigilant, manipulating others and ourselves as a way of protection. Now we literally don't know how to live life differently. Unfortunately, because we have become so encapsulated and narrow in our view of the world, we don't see what others can so readily see—that we have become authoritarian, demanding, inflexible, and perfectionistic.

We don't know how to listen. We cut people off in conversations and relationships. We don't ask for help. We can't see options. We have little spontaneity or reactivity. We experience psychosomatic health problems. We intimidate people by withholding our feelings. Blindly focused on our pursuit of safety, very often unaware of our emotional self and yet so frightened and full of shame, we rely on what we know best—control. But the consequences are almost the opposite of what we had hoped for. Our needs do not get met. Our relationships are out of balance. Ultimately, our hypervigilance becomes burdensome and exhausting. In our confusion about what has gone wrong when we have tried so hard to make things right, we succumb to depression and resort to unhealthy ways of coping with sadness and pain that often results in addictive behaviors.

Perfectionism

Perfectionism is driven by the belief that if a person's behavior is perfect there will be no reason to be criticized and therefore no reason for pain. Perfect children learn that no matter what they do, it's never good enough. As a result, in their struggle to feel good about themselves and relieve the source of pain, they constantly push to excel, to be the best at any cost, mostly for themselves.

Highly perfectionistic people are usually those who have been raised in a rigid home environment. The rigidity may be in the form of unrealistic expectations that parents have for their children and/or for themselves. In these situations, we internalize the parents' expectations. Rigidity may also be expressed as children feel the need to do things "right" in order to gain approval from their parent and to lessen fears of rejection. For most children, being "right" is perceived to mean there is no room for mistakes.

As children, we were taught to strive onward. There was never a time or place to rest or to have inner joy and satisfaction.

Perfection as a performance criterion means we never measure up. Then, not measuring up is translated into a comparison with others of good versus bad, better versus worse. Inevitably we end up feeling the lesser for the comparison. This comparison with others is one of the primary ways people continue to create more shame for themselves. We continue to do to ourselves on the inside what was done to us from the outside. Since our efforts were never experienced as sufficient, adequate, or good enough, we did not develop an internal sense of just how much is then good enough.

> *"I developed a perfectionist mind-set; anything short of being number one meant failure."*

Procrastination

Procrastination, such as starting but not completing a project, or considering a project but never initiating it, is often an attempt to defend against further shame. Perfectionism and procrastination are closely linked. Some people procrastinate because in the desire to do things perfectly, we recognize it will never be good enough or our efforts won't be acceptable, so we stop or we find safety in not trying.

For others, we received so little attention that we were not encouraged to initiate projects, let alone complete them. Too many times when we did something, drew a picture or wrote a story, and gleefully showed our mom or dad, our parents barely looked at it and then set it aside or maybe even lost it. When there is no positive reinforcement to complete school projects or homework, children perform with ambivalence. We believe "No one else cares" and develop the attitude "Why should I care?" The result is procrastination.

It is possible we were humiliated for our efforts, made to feel inadequate or stupid. When that happens we find ways to protect ourselves so we cease involvement in any action that would prove we really are a failure. In addition, we become discouraged when we are constantly compared to someone who did or might have done it better.

Tom says he was always compared to his two older brothers. "My two older brothers were articulate. They were quick and did well in school. It took me longer to grasp things. I wasn't as interested in math and sciences as they were. I was more interested in my friends. So, with school being more of a struggle and having no real help from my parents, only the push that 'you should be like your brothers,' I just gave up. I wasn't like them and didn't want to be."

Also mixed into procrastination can be anger, expressed as an attitude of "I'll show you—I won't finish this" or "I'll only do it part way. I won't give my best." Inherent in this attitude is a challenge that screams "Like me for who I am, not for what I do." In a family where rigidity is the rule, where it is not okay to make mistakes, not okay to take risks or be different, not okay to draw attention to yourself, we learn not to initiate or not to finish what we started. For those raised this way, it is amazing anything gets done.

> *"If I did something wrong while I was driving, my father would backhand me in the mouth. Needless to say, it wasn't easy to drive with tears, frustration, and anger. I had four learner's permits by the time I was eighteen. I was twenty-two before I had enough courage to get my license, and I was twenty-seven before I could drive on the freeway. I still get scared today to try new things. I put them off and in many cases I simply don't try."*

Victimization

When we have internalized beliefs, such as "I am not worthy," "I am not of value," "Other people are more important than me," or "Other people are more worthy," then it is difficult to set limits. We do not know how to say no. We struggle with appropriate boundaries and so often have no boundaries or damaged boundaries. It is a combination of not believing in our own worth and not developing the skills that go with a belief in our worthiness that leads to this victimization.

Victims have learned not to trust their own perceptions, believing that another person's perceptions are more accurate than their own. We always give others the benefit of the doubt and are willing to respond to the structure others set. Victims are not apt to question. In addition to the family rules Don't Talk, Don't Feel, Don't Trust, we have learned the rules Don't Question and Don't Think.

Not believing in our own worth, we often fail to realize that we even have needs and, as a result, do not take care of ourselves. We operate in a position of fear, unable to access any anger or indignation that comes with being hurt, disappointed, or even abused. When asked what we need or want, victims often literally do not know.

While the victim response is the result of the belief in personal powerlessness, it is clearly a response to the intense emotional pain. Not only is this an outcome of helplessness, it is also a kind of defense. We believe we may not have as much pain if we give in and relinquish autonomy to someone else.

Victims develop a high tolerance for pain and inappropriate behavior. We become emotionally separated from ourselves by becoming highly skilled at rationalizing, minimizing, and often flatly denying the events and emotions in our lives. We are not as readily able to identify others' behavior that has been hurtful because that would, in our perception, create a greater feeling of helplessness or invite more trouble.

Some victims stay in isolation. Those who choose to stay more visible often play victim/martyr roles: "Look at how I am victimized. Aren't they terrible for doing this to me! I will just have to endure." Being the victim becomes part of a cycle. Victims already feel bad about themselves as a result of being abandoned and/or used and abused. We don't act in a way that provides safety and security for ourselves, leading to greater abandonment or abuse.

Typically, the greater a person's shame, the more likely he or she will invite someone else with shame into his or her life. Very often, this other person is someone who appears to have the ability to take charge, make things happen, someone who feels strengthened by association with the victim's vulnerability. Depending on the specific history of the two people involved, that attraction often leads to the dominant one battering the victim, either emotionally or physically.

Almost inevitably, victims have great difficulty protecting themselves in the context of intimate relationships. For example, a person may have such a desperate longing for nurturance and care that it makes it difficult to establish safe and appropriate boundaries with others. We tend to belittle ourselves and to idealize those to whom we become attached, further clouding our judgment. This defensive style makes it difficult to accurately assess danger.

> *"I knew nothing about relationships. I didn't know what was appropriate to give in a relationship so I just gave, gave, and gave. I didn't know what my needs were. I didn't know how to ask for what I wanted. I didn't know*

what I wanted. I had learned no one really cared or was interested. My needs had never been met so I didn't expect that. So one relationship after the other, they were all alike. They took advantage of me; I have been slapped around a lot. I leave every relationship with less than I go in with."

For all of the reasons noted above, whether male or female, the shameful person is at great risk of repeated victimization.

"When I would hitchhike, guys would pick me up and not let me out until they got what they wanted. Then they would kick me out of the car and I'd put out my thumb again."

Rage

Rage is the holding tank for accumulated fears, angers, humiliations, and shame. It is intended to protect against further experiences of pain. It is a defense for no longer being able or willing to endure pain. Emotionally, it is an attempt to be heard, seen, and valued when we are most desperate and lacking in other skills. Rage is often behavior that compensates for an overwhelming sense of powerlessness. When we have lived with a chronic sense of helplessness combined with fear, rageful behavior offers us a sense of power. When rage is the only way people know to protect against emptiness, powerlessness, and pain, the choice is a quick one.

"In my rage I don't feel inadequate or defective. It may be a false sense of power I feel, but if all I have ever known is my powerlessness, I'll take false power over no power."

Rageful behavior also offers protection by keeping people at a distance. As a result, other people cannot see into the raging person's soul that he or she believes to be so ugly.

Many times people who are rageful grew up with rage. Therefore, it is often the only model one has for attempting to be heard or to garner control.

Rage as a defense also offers protection by transferring shame to others. The outwardly rageful person chooses a victimlike person who, consciously or not, is willing to take the abuse or assume the shame. We frequently live with people who become the chronic victim(s) of our rage; or we move around a lot, wearing out our welcome after relatively short periods of time in one place.

> *"I had always looked outside for the answers. My life was such a mess and everything I did was just making it worse. I had been so lonely, so frightened. I had felt so empty and didn't know why; alcohol and rage were my answers. And I became addicted to the high of both."*

Growing up, we may find anger to be the one safe feeling to express. This often leads to other vulnerabilities being masked with anger. Many people full of rage show no sign of other emotions. They keep a tight lid on all of their feelings until something triggers an eruption. There may be no signs of any feeling, and suddenly their rage is in someone else's face—this is what I refer to as "machine-gun bursts." Perhaps it is a scathing memo at work or an outburst of criticism toward a waiter or gas station attendant.

The rager is often the person best described as holding a gas can in one hand and a lit match in the other.

While some people outwardly show chronic rage, others live with an internalized, simmering anger—a silent rage. When anger is held back and internalized, it grows. It festers into chronic bitterness or chronic depression. When there has been no outlet for anger, it is more apt to explode suddenly as a significant single hostile act.

Examples of this are the highly publicized acts of school violence. Following the shootings in Jonesboro, Arkansas, West Paducah, Kentucky, and Springfield, Oregon, the teenaged shooters were all described as having shown no previous signs of aggression. After further investigation, however, it was discovered that these troubled boys carried burdens of buried rage, which became manifested in acts of deadly violence.

Even the two seniors at Columbine High School, responsible for killing twelve fellow students and a teacher before taking their own lives, were described by those who knew them as different but not overtly violent. In all these cases, however, the underlining message became clear: Outside appearance is not always a true indication of what is occurring on the inside.

Rageful behavior is not just the consequence of the accumulation of emotions. It is a combination of the inability to tolerate painful feelings and the inability to resolve conflict or to perceive options and choices. The latter, by themselves, are common consequences to growing up with addiction.

"While my mom was the one addicted to alcohol and drugs, my dad was addicted to his rage. He would fly off the handle at anything and everything. He would rant and rave and kill you with his words. He actually looked like he enjoyed it. The scenes were right out of a movie. Only they were very real for us. I swore I wouldn't end up like my dad, and yet that is exactly what I do today. I understand the high he got in his rage; I understand the power he felt. And it is destroying everything in my life."

Depression

Unfortunately, a depressed person is typically pictured as one who sleeps excessively, is unable to eat, and is suicidal. While that picture represents the severe end of the depression continuum, many depressed adults are able to function daily and meet most of their responsibilities. After all, that has been their survival mode. Remember, "looking good" children are often those who maintain the appearance of "doing just fine outside while dying slowly on the inside." Children in addictive homes develop the skill of compartmentalizing. We may have cried ourselves to sleep at night, or lashed out in anger, or hidden in fear, but when we got to school we didn't tell anyone about our feelings or experiences. We presented ourselves to the world as "We are fine, life is fine, and nothing is amiss." We presented a false self that may not have had the look of depression, while our true self, our emotional and spiritual self, was experiencing great despair. We practiced this day in and out, week after week, month after month, and year after year. It easily became a skill and we took it with us into various areas of our lives. As a consequence, many adult children do not demonstrate blatant depression but are a part of the walking wounded, the "closeted depressed."

To keep depression hidden, those of us who are depressed avoid sharing with others on an intimate level or avoid spending enough time with friends who may recognize our true feelings and our internal despair or emptiness. We often rely on defenses of busyness and accomplishing tasks. We deliberately keep the focus on other things and other people. We appear very capable and put out an impenetrable force field that says, "Don't ask me about myself. Don't push me."

It is difficult enough being depressed. It is even more difficult when we have shame around it—shame as one cause of depression and added shame because we are depressed.

Depression is complex and addressed in a variety of ways. For many it is a biochemical imbalance or disordered neurochemistry, best treated with antidepressants. It is commonly accepted among professionals that depression tends to run in families, suggesting there may be a physiological predisposition towards depression. But chemical depression is also induced by external experiences. For many, it is a consequence of a habitually pessimistic and disordered way of viewing the world. Living with addiction certainly allows one to see the world in a negative and chaotic manner. It frequently is also the consequence of loss and the inability to do the grief work necessary to bring completion to the feelings of sorrow. It can be referred to as pathological grief. The latter most often fuels closeted depression.

NOTE: All depression needs to be assessed by a qualified physician.

There is tremendous loss associated with being raised in a shame-based family. With the family being denial-centered, as it often is, and it not being okay to talk honestly, the sense of loss is amplified because there is no way to work through the pain. The hurt, the disappointment, the fears, and the angers associated with life events are all swirled together and internalized. When we add to this a personal belief that says, "I am at fault" or "I am not worthy," it is easy to see why we came to believe in our unworthiness and so try to hide our real self from others. Eventually, whether we are thirty-five or fifty-five, we suddenly hit a wall. The burden of hiding eventually becomes too heavy and all of those protecting, controlling mechanisms that kept us going for so long just stop working. Depression either sets in or our ability to compartmentalize is so diminished that we are no longer able to hide our depression.

"I didn't even know I was depressed until I was no longer depressed. I had always lived like this. I functioned. I operated in the world. I had a good job, family. But I have never felt joy. Oh, I am very socially skilled; no one

knew how I felt over the years. Then one day, I just couldn't keep the pretenses up. None of my old defenses kept working. It was like I hit a wall I did not see coming."

Depression and Addiction

Depression frequently becomes masked with addictive disorders. Today we are recognizing that when people become clean and sober from their various addictions there is often a clinical depression strongly fueled from years of shame, pain, and powerlessness. In theory, an addictive relationship can be established with just about anything, as long as the substance, person, or activity relieves the threat of overt depression. To accomplish this, the defense frequently transforms one's emotional state from shame to grandiosity, from feelings of worthlessness to feelings of extraordinary worth and well-being. The addiction always pulls the person from "less than" to "better than." Along with the obvious effect of drugs or alcohol, one can also get "high" from the rush of physical violence, the applause of an audience, a sexual conquest, or a killing in the stock market. Socialization of men in general pushes them toward arousal-type behaviors.

Some people are only looking for an escape from their pain, their shame, their depression. They seek what is referred to as satiation drugs, such as alcohol, sedatives, or compulsive overeating. There are both satiating and risk-taking arousal behaviors within the various addictions. Certain acts of gambling are more sedating, such as slot machines; others more arousing, such as horse racing or day trading. Some sexual behaviors are acts of sedation and calming, and others involve the arousal of risk. Compulsive overeating is most frequently a sedating response to the helplessness and the shame associated with depression.

As a society, we have more respect for the walking wounded, those who deny their difficulties, creating a need for people to mask their depression. The combination of socialization, plus the addictive upbringing, creates even greater shame for men around the issues of feelings. It should be no surprise that men are four times more likely to take their own lives than women. Culturally men are also encouraged and expected to engage in risk-taking behaviors. As a result, men, even more so than women, will frequently mask their depression with addiction.

By the time many adult children show obvious (overt) depression it is usually little more than the final eruption of a long-term chronic, closeted, hidden depression.

Addictive Disorders

"I can remember my first drink. I was eleven. I hated the taste, but I felt the glow and it worked. I would get sick as a dog and then swear on a stack of Bibles I would not do it again, but I kept going back. I got drunk because I had a hole in my gut so big, and alcohol and then other drugs would fill the hole. They became the solution."

When we come from a pain-based family we frequently go outside of ourselves for a quick answer to relieve our suffering. Relief from this intolerable pain must come, one way or another. We need someone or something to take away our profound loneliness and fear, and so we seek a mood-altering experience. We need to escape. And when we grow up in an environment of shame, where the cause of pain is external, we develop the belief that the solutions to problems exist only externally through substances or behaviors that are medicators.

Substance addictions may include dependency on food, particularly sugars or starches, caffeine, nicotine, alcohol, and other drugs. With the exception of illicit drugs, these are substances that are an integral part of our culture, socially sanctioned and supported, making it very difficult for the abuser to recognize initially how they are using them in unhealthy ways.

In addition to temporarily controlling our pain, the substances we use and abuse very often provide something for us we do not know how to seek naturally. As an example, alcohol may give a sense of power to someone who has known only powerlessness. It may give access to courage and confidence to someone who feels lacking. This is certainly drug-induced, temporary, and false, but for many people, false courage is better than none. For someone who is isolated and feels alienated, alcohol makes it easier to reach out to people. "Give me a little bit to drink and I become alive. I pull myself away from the wall and I find myself talking, laughing, and listening. I see people responding to me and I like it." This kind of thinking doesn't mean that a person is addicted, but it does mean he or she is thirsty for connection with others. In this case alcohol becomes the reinforcement in order to feel whole and complete.

For people who have never taken time for play or laughter because life has been so serious, alcohol gives them the opportunity to relax. Alice identified, "My entire life has been spent taking care of other people. I am always busy. I make these lists daily, thinking the world will stop if I don't get the job done. I don't think about missing out on fun—it has never been a part of my life. I never drank until I was twenty-six. I don't even know why I started. Those first few times I heard myself laugh with other people it actually scared me. I remember thinking that I was being silly. Yet at the same time there was this attraction. It was as if there was this whole other part of me I didn't know and maybe was okay to know. The attraction to relaxing with alcohol kept getting stronger. I can actually remember thinking, *I don't have to make this decision tonight* or *I don't have to do this by myself.* Pretty soon it was *I don't have to do this at all.* I was having fun. I was relaxing."

Because Alice did not know how to relax without alcohol, she ultimately became dependent on it. She, like so many others, was seeking wholeness. But the only glimpse she had of it was "under the influence."

Addictive behaviors, whether they are substance abuses or process addictions, give us those things we have not learned to acquire naturally, such as courage, confidence, laughter, power, and control, or they lessen those parts of us that frighten us—our emotions. Common process addictions range from compulsive activities, such as gambling, spending of money, and sexual behaviors, to relationship dependencies and work addiction. We may even be compulsively busy. We can use any and all of these to distance or distract ourselves, to get our minds off our pain, our fear, or our anger. They allow us to stay in control of our feelings and therefore to avoid feeling bad, or they may represent how out of control we genuinely are in our lives. Many behavioral compulsions would be otherwise harmless activities if they weren't exaggerated, destroying the balance in our lives. For example, exercise is a healthy activity until done so excessively that we actually injure our bodies. Addiction is about living in the extreme without a sense of moderation.

As Felicia said, "Food was love; food was attention. It was a way to connect with my dad and break away from and rebel against my mom. Food was the answer. It was the solution and my friend. It was about control. I didn't learn to control or manage my food. All I learned was how to rebel, to sneak, and to be dishonest."

Starving ourselves, purging, and compulsive overeating may be anger turned toward ourselves. We may be punishing ourselves for being bad. The anorexic may be literally starving herself to become invisible in response to shame; the anorexic and bulimic may be seeking perfection—which is based in shame.

"By fourth grade I was preoccupied with food. I told myself in a proud way that I was addicted to Coca-Cola, just like Mom was addicted to booze."

"Caffeine and chocolate have been my breakfast for years."

Relationship addiction is the dependence on being in a relationship to validate our worth. We use our relationship as proof of our worthiness. We use other people to lessen our shame and to avoid truly facing ourselves. To be outside of a relationship is too frightening. To be alone often puts us in touch with our emptiness, what we interpret to be our lack of value. Being in a relationship allows us to be focused on others, not having to focus on our own pain. The problem with this is we often tolerate hurtful behavior, don't assert ourselves, and don't grow within a relationship. We will go to any lengths to maintain or get into a relationship at the price of our own well-being.

As surprising as it is for the person involved, it is common for children raised with substance abuse to marry (often times more than once) a substance abuser or someone with another type of addiction. In addition to how adult child issues fuel the potential for relationship addiction, other factors are:

- Due to age, we are more likely to meet our partner when he or she is in the earlier stages of their addictive disorder. Very possibly, we did not know our parent when they were at that similar age. By the time we are old enough for memory, our parent is into the middle or even later stages of their addiction so we do not recognize it in the early stage.

- Not understanding addiction in general and only having a family frame of reference. The person we partner with is addicted to a different substance or behavior than the one we were raised with so we don't see the blatant similarities. To assure ourselves we don't marry someone like our parent, who was alcoholic, we may marry someone who drinks very little or not at all. But, lo and behold, they end up being addicted to cocaine or another drug, or they have a gambling problem, sex addiction, or other addictive process.
- We recognize our partner has a problem, but we tell ourselves we can handle it. We have handled our parent's problem, and we can handle this as well. We believe we have the advantage of knowing what to expect, and we tell ourselves *With this person it will not be so bad.* Impoverished expectations, denial, and low self-worth interfere with making healthy choices.

Sex addiction is the use of sexual stimulation to act as a detractor or medicator of pain. It may also be a false way of accessing power to overcome a sense of powerlessness. Compulsive sex experiences can temporarily offer warmth and an appearance of love. Or they can be an expression of anger. These experiences may temporarily affirm that we are lovable and worthy, all the while compounding our belief in our defectiveness. Sex addicts vary in their focus from obsessive masturbating, the use of pornographic materials, exhibitionism, obscene phone calls, and voyeurism to multiple affairs, use of prostitutes, and so on. For the addict, the sexual experience is the source of nurturing, focus of energy, and origin of excitement. It is the remedy for pain and anxiety, the reward for success, and the means for maintaining emotional balance.

"There was so much pain I was forever seeking ways to escape. As a child it was food, fantasy reading, and television. I was always looking for someplace safe. I never felt safe. I never felt good about myself or even adequate. I was never enough. I know that is what my sex addiction is about. By paying for women they will not reject me. They are safe. I get consumed with the ritual of finding them; it's me in a fantasy world again. All the

pressures I feel, the anxiety that for me comes with living, are gone. Then I go back to my guilt and shame, but with even more, and then I venture back to the hunt."

Our relationships with money are often distorted and many people find compulsive spending or gambling addictions as their external solution. Denise has experienced serious repetitive credit card debt due to compulsively shopping. Somehow having multiple amounts of everything makes her feel less empty and more complete. She has closets full of shopping bags that have never even been opened.

"Spending money gives me a sense of power. For just a little while it can feel so great."

"When I gamble I feel a rush. I feel I hold the world in my hand. My concentration is so focused, every past, present, or future problem is obliterated from my reality!"

Even though compulsive behaviors distract and alter feelings, a feeling itself can become compulsive in nature. We become dependent on certain emotions to mask and avoid what we are really experiencing. We may become a rage-aholic, using rage as a release for all feelings. Fear can overwhelm us; phobias, hypervigilance, and anxieties can control our lives.

While some compulsions are certainly more harmful to ourselves and our family, others may be considered only nuisances. Yet any time we use a substance or become involved in a process or behavior that interferes with our honesty, our ability to be present with ourselves, it deserves our attention.

Suicide

"I am hopeless. I am unworthy and I don't deserve to live. Life won't get any better and I can't stand this pain."

Suicidal thoughts, attempts, and completions speak of many issues. They are often a reflection of anger, rage turned inward, and depression. For some people, the act of suicide seems to grant power that compensates for the powerlessness in their life. For others, death is perceived to be a better option than living with certain memories and shame. The pain is too overwhelming, and out of despair and hopelessness, people become their own victims. Thoughts of taking our own lives are much more prevalent than people realize. While pain creates such thoughts, we also experience shame for having the thoughts. My message to you is

Please speak up and let someone know how frightened, angry, or hopeless you are feeling.

When you are considering suicide as a way out of your pain, you must reach out and get assistance from a helping professional. In recovery, you can speak about those issues that have created the pain. You can say "No" to your shame. You can learn to find ways to express your anger without hurting yourself. You can develop new beliefs and behaviors that support you in the way you deserve to be supported. You can learn how to access the power within you that does exist. You deserve to be able to live without pain.

Rage, depression, victimization, addictions, compulsions, perfectionism, and procrastination—these are some of the responses to having lived with fear and pain. Other responses might be intellectualization, physical isolation, humor, magical thinking, lying, silence, or withdrawal. It is important to be empathetic to why such defenses were created but to no longer deny the negative impact they have on life today. These protectors begin as common, everyday acts, but taken to extremes create negative outcomes in the long run.

Chapter 6

Family Violence

"We never knew when he would blow up, or for what, and who would be the target of his anger. He would suddenly threaten one of us for no reason at all. His favorite saying was, 'This is my house, and I'll do what I want.'"

For many, living in an addictive family means to live with both physical and sexual abuses, to be the witness of the abuse or to be the direct recipient of it.

In January of 1999, a 167-page report from the National Center on Addiction and Substance Abuse at Columbia University said, "There is no safe haven for abused and neglected children of drug and alcohol abusing parents. They are the most vulnerable and endangered individuals in America. In dollars, parental substance abuse and addiction costs the nation some $10 billion in federal, state and local child welfare system costs." It would go on to say that substance abuse causes or exacerbates seven out of ten cases of child abuse or neglect. Children whose parents abuse drugs and alcohol are three times more likely to be abused and four times more likely to be neglected than children whose parents are not substance abusers. My own research indicates that 66 percent of children raised in alcoholic families have been physically abused or have witnessed abuse of another family member. In more than one-third of these families, such abuse occurs on a regular basis.

Continuum of Physical Abuse

Because people who have been raised in abusive families have a high tolerance for inappropriate behavior and violence, it is often helpful to describe abusive behavior.

When we think of physical abuse, we often picture a badly beaten, chronically black-and-blue child. In reality, battering may be much more subtle and infrequent, with barely visible results. Battering can occur in the form of pushing and shoving, grabbing, pinching, or choking. It may be slapping, hitting, kicking, punching, or slamming a person against the wall, to the floor, against the car.

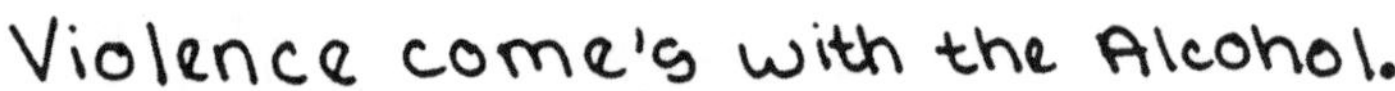

But abuse can be emotional as well as verbal or physical. In many addictive homes, only terror exists; no bruises attesting to violence are evident. Children and spouses frequently experience intensely frightening and physically dangerous situations. When Dad, in an alcoholic siege, takes the family for a sixty-miles-per-hour car ride down a mountain road at night with the headlights turned off, the effect is just as traumatic as any physical violence, yet it leaves no physical scars. Michael describes his mother's rages, "I can still see my mom throwing dishes, and I can hear her yelling at us kids things we should never have heard. She would chase us with a knife, threatening to kill us if she caught us."

For some, the trauma is in the witnessing of physical abuse of siblings or the other parent—which is often more damaging than receiving the abuse itself.

"I would be terrified. The voices were loud, and sometimes my mother would throw things. I pretended I heard nothing. I would be terrified that

something awful would happen. Sometimes the police would come, sometimes the neighbors. When it got really bad, my mother would come, pull me out of bed, and tell me to pack. I would obey. We would leave. This became routine."

"My father would always beat my mother when he was drunk. Then he got so he beat my brother. I hated it. Then I got so I tried to interfere and be a referee to prevent the arguing that would lead to the violence. But one night he threw me onto a chair, told me to shut up or I'd get the bottle right across my face. I tried to speak up but quickly shut up. He would have done it. After that, I could only watch. I hated him, but even more I hated me for my powerlessness and fear."

What actually goes on in the day-to-day existence of one who lives in the shadow of physical violence is often beyond the imagination of those who have never had such an experience.

"When Dad drank, someone got beat. We hated to see him get started, but the quarreling was awful loud. My mom was hurt a lot. How did he get started on me? Simple. I defended my mom and if he wanted to know who did something, rather than see my younger brother or sisters get it, I did it! No matter what it was. He usually used a wooden hanger or Marine belt on us. I still look out for my brother and sisters and my mom; I wouldn't lift a finger to help my dad. I refused to go to his funeral or send flowers. I am the same with my own kids, take care of them, protect them from my ex-husband, who somehow has managed to develop a dependency on prescription drugs, always has a beer in his hand, and likes to hit."

Andrea has a similar story: "My mother taught me that at all costs I should never do anything to make my father angry. I lived in constant fear of his awful silence that could at the most unexpected moment turn into a red-faced rage. I have a mental picture of myself in a crouch, like a dog that looks pleadingly, hoping not to be beaten up, but expecting it, hoping to please the master but knowing it will never happen. The master will not—cannot—be pleased."

Neglect

"My parents didn't have to beat us; the neglect did it for them."

Neglect is another form of abuse in addictive families. It is demonstrated with inadequate supervision, such as leaving young children in the care of other children nearly as young as themselves or leaving children with no supervision at all.

Neglect is also inadequate physical care, such as not providing meals or proper clothing and shelter. Such children often describe never knowing when dinner is. "It could be anywhere from 6 p.m. to midnight. It would range from Chinese take-out food to hot dogs or ice cream."

> *"Food was on a first-come, first-served basis. That meant I often went hungry because there was never enough food for us. We would grab from the stove and take it anywhere in the house. If our parents were really angry with us or really drunk, we didn't eat at all."*

Children often have clothes that are too small or inadequate for the weather, such as thin coats or simply sweaters to withstand rain and snow. Neglect is also inadequate medical attention. Marti described, "My mother's way of coping was to ignore everything, thinking it would go away. She did this with both my diabetes and my father's violent rages."

> *"I didn't question all of the drinking because I had to spend so much time responding to the abuse. The neglect was okay, at least then they weren't deliberately hurting you."*

The neglect may be so pervasive that children learn to not question or challenge it. It is often only as we hear others talk and receive feedback that we begin to realize the extent of deprivation in our lives.

Dynamics of Abuse

While addiction and battering are not always related, it is helpful to examine similarities in the dynamics of both when experienced in the home. When they coexist and interact, the dynamics are simply multiplied.

Both the batterer and the addict:

- minimize and deny their abusive behaviors.
- discount their acts and minimize the severity of their drunkenness or battering.
- blame others, neither will accept the responsibility for their behavior.
- exhibit Jekyll-and-Hyde personality changes. Children may experience an overly nice, caring parent who after taking a few drinks becomes a raging lion. In this case, the batterer simply erupts like a volcano for what appears to be no apparent reason.
- rationalize their behavior, and invariably, there is (in their own rationale) a good reason (excuse) for the drinking or for the violent behavior. Episodic violence and drinking occur more and more frequently as these unhealthy lifestyles progress. Inevitably, for the alcoholic and the batterer, the drinking and the violence begin to cause more trauma and more problems in almost all areas of family and personal life.
- increasingly feel more guilt and remorse.
- make promises and create false hopes.
- continue this cycle indefinitely, unless they seek treatment.

Spouses and children:

- minimize the impact of the drinking and/or using and violence in the family. This is the family's denial process. The dysfunctional family rules of Don't Feel, Don't Trust, and Don't Talk permeate the family. Addiction, when coupled with violence, doubles the need for denial and creates an even greater sense of helplessness in the lives of family members. When children don't show obvious signs of being emotionally affected by violence, it is important to recognize that it is probably due to denial. Children in battered families develop an almost identical denial process as the children in addictive homes. When addiction and battering coexist, they practice denial to a greater extent.
- accept the blame because they believe that had they been better in their roles (a better wife, or a better child) the batterer/alcoholic would have no reason to get so upset, fly into rages, and drink or use.

Children are naturally inexperienced and vulnerable. They have no frame of reference from which they can make judgments and tend to believe anything they are told. Their own sense of confusion makes them quick to accept blame for any given situation. They naturally feel powerless in dealing with grown-ups, see themselves as unable to protect themselves, and do not perceive themselves as having available resources to protect them.

Role patterns in the violent home are often similar to those seen in addictive homes, only with an even greater intensity when both problems coexist. There is one significant difference between homes plagued with addiction and those with violence. Addiction usually manages to reveal itself to others outside the home, whereas family violence is much more hidden from those not living in the home. The goal of family members in attempting to live through these problems is the same—minimize the conflict, adjust, placate, act out, drop out—do anything just to survive.

Cause and Effect

While research is not showing that alcohol and other drugs are the direct cause of abuse, it does substantiate that they are a significant contributing factor. Also, it cannot be assumed that the addicted parent is always the abuser. The abusing parent may very well be the nonaddicted parent. When this is true, the addicted parent is so caught up in their disease they are often oblivious to the abuse, the child, or just too incapacitated to intervene. When the addict is the abuser, the other parent frequently does not respond due to his or her own victimized role. When the abusers are the addicted parent(s), abuse doesn't necessarily occur when they are drinking or using. In fact, sometimes it is when the addict is not under the influence that they may be abusive. We also know that when a child has two chemically dependent parents, the likelihood of physical abuse becomes even greater, and the likelihood of both parents abusing increases. Sibling abuse also increases within an addictive family. Brothers and sisters may terrorize each other. When this occurs it is most likely the older children who become the abusers of the younger children in the home. The predominant model they have for their painful feelings is to attack someone less powerful—a younger brother or sister.

"While Dad's drinking increased, Mom became more erratic. She was playful and fun one moment and full of rage the next. She would pick up anything (whip, vacuum cleaner hose, spoon) and hit and hit and hit, and would never apologize. Even when we were bleeding, somehow it was still our fault."

Sexual Abuse

"I am apprehensive talking about this problem because I am afraid others might find out. I was seven when my dad began to touch me and make me touch and kiss him. He did a lot of things to me. It hurt. He used to threaten me that he would do the same thing to my younger sisters if I told. I didn't know what to do when I was eighteen so I stayed home another year. He died in a drinking-and-driving accident. Then I left home, never telling anyone. Years later I found out he had been molesting my sisters all of this time too. I am only now beginning to accept my past and present family situations. I withdraw from people when afraid because I think they might hurt me. I don't visit my mother or sisters. I feel guilty for never going home. I've always felt guilty."

Twenty-five million children under the age of eleven live in homes where they are sexually abused. Incest occurs in many homes and in all socioeconomic classes. While research concerning sexual abuse and its relationship to addictive disorders is limited, and varies in its conclusions, a number of studies document that over 50 percent of known incest victims lived in homes where alcohol abuse was a major problem. In addition, many private practitioners report 60 percent to 80 percent of the addicted women they treat are sexual abuse survivors. My own research indicates 26 percent of females and 16 percent of males in alcoholic homes have been sexual abuse victims.

Sexual abuse is inappropriate sexual behavior, usually perpetrated by an adult with a minor child, and brought about by coercion, deception, or psychological manipulation. While some victims are infants and others are in their late teens, research is saying that most females are initially approached between the ages of five and eight, with the sexual abuse being incestuous activity usually continuing for a minimum of three years.

There is much less information available about sexual abuse of males. My clinical experience does report a difference. Females most frequently report sexual abuse to be continuous and within the home, while males report more sexual abuse occurs outside of the home and is often a "one time only" incident or occurs over a short duration of time. It is not uncommon for males to report "one time only" incidents with different perpetrators.

Sexual abuse also occurs on a continuum. Psychological sexual abuse involves an adult telling details about his or her sex life to a child, flirting, acting jealous, or in some other way manipulating a child's emotions. It occurs when daughters are treated like wives or girlfriends and sons are treated like husbands or boyfriends. Psychological abuse, also referred to as covert sexual abuse, includes inappropriate touching that appears to be accidental, an adult's habit of walking into the bathroom while a child or teenager is showering, or seductive comments about a child's developing body. Overt abuse involves kissing, displaying one's naked body to a child in order to get a sexual response, oral sex, anal sex, and penetration.

Perpetrators seldom commit childhood sexual abuse to solely satisfy their own sexual needs. It is an act of violence and selfishness and it is a violation of a position of trust, power, and protection. They do it to exercise power over someone. And it thrives in silence. Abusers use power, age, experience, and position to persuade, coerce, bribe, and threaten their victims into doing things they are not old enough or emotionally mature enough to cope with or defend against. The perpetrator takes advantage of the child's emotional, social, or financial dependence on him or her. If the person who becomes sexual with the child is even just a few years older than the child, or holds a position of power or authority, it is molestation; if the person is related to the child it is incest. Both constitute sexual abuse.

Even if the victim doesn't try to stop it, the child is not responsible for the sexual abuse. Remember, a child who is the victim of sexual abuse usually has no place to escape to and is too frightened to tell. Children are too young and immature to make the kinds of decisions that are involved in this type of sexual behavior. It is the responsibility and the fault of the older, more powerful person.

Children don't talk about the sexual abuse for many of the same reasons they don't talk about the addiction. The onset, so many times, is very gradual and children may not even recognize what is happening until the behavior has been repeated for some time. By then, children have often developed guilt feelings. The victims don't talk because of fear. Fear that they will not be believed: "She (Mom) wouldn't have believed me" or "She wouldn't have done anything about it anyway." "That might have hurt more, and that would kill me," one woman responded. Another women revealed, "I do remember being really scared, like I shouldn't be doing this—but he was my father. You listen to your father. I did it because he wanted me to do it; it was expected of me. You don't argue in my family. No one has rights in my family until you are out of the house and self-supporting."

It is common for victims to become confused about the abuse when they were not physically forced to comply. Perpetrators often play on trust to coerce their victim into meeting their demands. It is well known that abusers often choose children starving for attention, warmth, and affection. Children from troubled families are prime victims because they are particularly desperate for any sign of attention and affection. Susanne described her stepfather as the only father she knew. Her biological father had no contact with the family. Her stepfather was the primary parent in the family. He frequently fixed the dinner and helped the children with their homework, while her mother was often at school, out with friends, or simply not wanting to do those things at home. So when he began to give her long hugs and then back rubs, it seemed to be just another way of his attending to her. When he ultimately wanted her to touch him sexually, she said she was not scared, it was just being nice to him for being so good to her.

When Danny's molestation began at the age of ten, he said he also liked the attention. He said his friend's father took him to the ball games, gave him money, and that the molestation didn't hurt and felt good. At home he didn't know when his dad would be raging next. His father never affectionately touched him or said anything nice to him so he gravitated to the father figure who showed him attention.

Sexual abuse is an insidious type of violence that often does not require physical force. However, that does not mean the victim wanted it to happen. Susanne and Danny wanted the affection and they liked the attention. They did not realize they were being taken advantage of, they did not initially realize they were being victimized.

The victims are often afraid the family will break up if they don't go along with what the perpetrator wants. The addictive family is already on such shaky ground that children are terrified of losing the little stability they still have. They feel that if the family were to break up they would be responsible for it.

Not trusting one's own feelings is experienced at an early age in an addictive family. The feeling is exaggerated when addiction is coupled with incest. Often, if the child challenges the appropriateness of the perpetrator's sexual activity, the perpetrator deceives the child by convincing them that the behavior is acceptable. The child is often manipulated into feeling guilty for questioning the molester's behavior or may possibly be threatened. The child begins to believe their perceptions are faulty so will succumb to the demands. The youngster becomes intimidated and readily assumes the guilt and responsibility for the "bad" feelings. The child learns extremely well how to discount their perceptions and develops a sense of powerlessness.

"I didn't tell anybody about it. I was about eight when it started. I had a vague idea it was something bad, but I didn't know what sex was. I only knew the way he acted was something I didn't want to be part of. I would try to avoid getting into those situations. I would come home from school late hoping Mom would get home first. I made up excuses not to go places alone with him. But, once it began, I just sort of passively sat there. I wouldn't talk to him, and when he let me go, I would get out of there as quickly as possible. I never told anyone what he was doing. Oftentimes when he came into my bedroom I thought if I pretended I was asleep he would go away, and I really didn't want to acknowledge that it was happening."

In addition, victims often fear they will not be believed if they tell. That could well be true, for this is already a family where telling the truth is not supported. People in the addictive family are busy rationalizing and minimizing other people's hurtful, neglectful, or inappropriate behavior. People are not held accountable for their behavior and blaming is more common. It is not uncommon to hear of a sexual abuse survivor who has told a parent about someone attempting to or actually molesting them and that parent reacts punitively, as if the child is putting one more burden on the parent to handle. The parent doesn't want to believe that their partner or extended family member or neighbor would do such a thing. It is easier to blame a child and accuse them of looking for attention and lying than to face something that seems so overwhelming and shaming. Unfortunately, the dynamics of the family are often such that the needs of the adult supercede the needs of a child. There is often immaturity of a parent that doesn't allow them to listen, prioritize the needs of, or protect their child.

If this weren't enough, the perpetrator often threatens to hurt or even kill the victim, another family member, or a pet if the child tells about the abuse. These are children who already feel false guilt for the conflict or unspoken pain in the family. This is just one more threatening consequence of asking for help or telling the truth.

Children from addictive families are less able to defend themselves against their offenders because of the dynamics of growing up with addiction. These children:

- have greater difficulty identifying their feelings.
- have a greater fear in trusting their own perceptions and trusting others.
- are more confused about what constitutes appropriate boundaries.
- have an existing base of shame as a result of living with the dynamics of addiction. Shame upon shame fuels powerlessness, making it more difficult for this child to reach out for help.
- have had to deal with a wall of denial when they attempt to discern the truth about what is going on in their lives.
- have had to deal with a sense of powerlessness over the addiction. This is compounded by a sense of total powerlessness over their own bodies.
- have learned that there is no safe place for them. They are locked in because there is no way for them to confront their offenders. Confrontation means shame, guilt, denial, abandonment, and possibly physical violence.
- see no way to break out of the cycle of abuse.

Sexual abuse is an overwhelming, damaging, and humiliating assault on a child's mind, soul, and body.

Legacy of Family Violence

"Dad was a great teacher, and I was his prize pupil. I picked up all of his self-centeredness, dishonesty, demanding, false promises, his addiction, and his outright abusive behavior, plus all of the guilt, remorse, and low self-esteem that goes with it. I had always sworn I'd never be like Dad—but ultimately I got there."

Physical Abuse

If your great-grandfather, your grandfather, and your father had red hair, there is a strong probability that you have red hair and your children will too. Addictive disorders and abuse are similar. They too can pass from generation to generation. Though not all addicts learn their drinking and using behavior at their parents' knees, children frequently imitate the styles of their parents. While not all abusers learn their behavior in their parents' homes, the overwhelming tendency is to punish as we were punished, to resolve conflict the way we saw it resolved, to construct our relationships as our parents did, and to continue to tolerate the levels of abuse we learned in childhood.

When addiction and abuse occur together, the issues are multiplied. For example, if the child (young or adult) has a difficult time trusting others, the child who was raised with both addiction and violence will experience a lack of trust to a greater degree. If the child has a hard time knowing what he or she feels, the child raised with both issues may experience not being able to identify their feelings to a greater degree. Just as we comment to ourselves or others *it will never happen to me*, convinced we will not become addicted or ever marry someone who is addicted, we do that with violence as well. Anger burns out of control in abusive families. As a result the child is usually someone who becomes anger avoidant, terrified of any anger, theirs or others, or they, too, become abusive in their anger. We frequently marry someone who is chronically angry or even rageful, or we become abusive in our own anger.

"I would have private temper tantrums. I'd throw things, slam doors, and swear a lot. I'd become enraged at the slightest frustration—getting stuck

in traffic or losing my keys and not being able to get the door open. All the things I'd locked in as a child were slowly slipping out."

"I was a strict disciplinarian. I would spank and then lose control. I always responded to whatever my kids did in a physical way. Afterward I would be so appalled by what I had done. Even more so, I was appalled I was just like my father. I felt mortified with shame. But I couldn't seem to stop myself, and the beatings continued."

"I was so afraid of any conflict, any anger, I'd do anything to placate, to please my husband, but in reality that did very little to stop his rage."

For the person raised with violence, the self-hate is overwhelming. Low self-esteem, coupled with a pervasive sense of powerlessness and fear of conflict, often compels someone to choose a partner who also has low self-esteem and acts out their low self-worth in a similar manner. The person raised with violence has internalized the words and behavior that repetitively told them they were worthless; they were not deserving; they would never amount to anything; or they couldn't do anything right. They frequently succumb to depression, believing in their helplessness and hopelessness. Others resort to addictive behaviors. Many become abusers.

Sexual Abuse

The combination of the physical act of being victimized, improper role modeling and nurturing, and feelings of fear, guilt, and anger leads to severe depression and/or delinquent behaviors. As a child, Cindy used drugs, promiscuity, and then razor blades for self-mutilation. Josh used alcohol and Valium and made several suicide attempts beginning at the age of nine. Amy resorted to compulsive overeating, then compulsive masturbation, and then finally anorexia. The list goes on. Eating disorders, substance abuse, depression, suicide attempts, and sexual acting out lead many people into their own sexual addiction, sexual offending, or victimization.

Confusion about trust and sexuality combined with role patterns and dynamics of not talking, not trusting, and not feeling often cause victims to repeat these psychological dynamics in adulthood.

Alice was sexually abused by her father, her brothers, and then her brother's friends. She was having sex with any guy she knew by the time she was fourteen. "I was fourteen and all I knew about myself was I could do two things well. One was to drink and the other was to get a guy to bed. They were my points of pride." Often sex is the only way one knows to get attention because it is basically the only way they were ever given attention. Sexual abuse survivors learned to be validated and have personal power through being sexual. The promiscuity is a misguided search for love, nurturing, and acceptance, but it does not work.

It is easy to be involved in sexually abusive relationships when one's sexual boundaries have been repeatedly violated. As the survivor feels dirty and doesn't know how to say no, more shame is incorporated, greater helplessness is experienced, and then more repetition occurs.

Josh, raised by two chemically dependent parents, experienced more covert sexual abuse by his father and more blatant abuse by his mother. His father wouldn't allow the boys to wear nightclothes and wandered the house nude and drunk. He teased the boys mercilessly about their sexual development. His dad often drank outside of the home, leaving Josh home alone with his mother where she did her drinking. The older brothers were often out on the streets. "I needed love and attention from my mom, but then she'd go into this striptease and molest me. I wanted her to stop, but I didn't know how. I felt so powerless. I thought I should have known what to do, how to get myself out of this situation. I should have been a grown-up and done the right thing. I had this terrible sense of shame because I didn't know what to do. I didn't know how to get away from my pain."

While many children in addictive homes do not experience physical sexual violation, the consequences are there for those who experience the more covert or emotional forms of sexual abuse. A twenty-six-year-old woman discussed her adolescent fears of believing she would be sexually violated. She was so sure of the possibility she had begun to take a knife to her bedroom to defend and protect herself from an anticipated attack.

She described her confusion as a result of the increasingly changing behavior patterns evidenced by her father. He changed from a caring, fun-loving father to a blaming, harsh, verbally abusive, drunken stranger. This child became more fearful of her father's actions when, along with his alcohol-induced behavior, he began talking about how "bad" it was for girls to be sexual. He became increasingly graphic in his descriptions and began accusing the women in the family of misconduct in their sexual behavior. He demonstrated growing hostility toward the young girl's boyfriends. Eventually, he began visiting her room late at night to accuse her of sexual activity with boys. Her fear of possible sexual abuse by her father coupled with the normal love a child feels for a father led to a great sense of confusion and shame about her own sexuality. For three years she took a knife to bed, hid it under a pillow, and took herself through a visualization where she let go of any positive feelings for her father and told herself she would kill him if he touched her. He never touched her. But she would carry the emotional scars of the terror and shame she felt, and she would carry the skill of dissociating from her feelings into her adult life.

While it is undoubtedly more hurtful to be raped than to be sexually teased, any abuse can wound a person's sense of self and sexuality. The damage includes feeling that one is powerless and has no say in relationships, lack of good judgment about relationships, reluctance to trust, fear of intimacy, inability to stay mentally present during sex, fear of sex, or shame about one's body and being a man or woman.

It is obvious that adults who drink and abuse drugs are not proper role models for children, particularly during the time when healthy attitudes regarding sexuality need to be learned. Drug-affected and impaired parents often speak crudely or tease children inappropriately with sexual innuendoes. In some homes, children are forced to deal with the drunken nudity of a parent; in other homes, parents make no attempt at maintaining discreet sex lives. The children very often face these problems alone, in silence, confused and feeling needless shame.

Nativity

Red hood drapes his black robe's back candles subdue the sanctuary, Noel Noel we sing.

At midnight he stands before us rolling down the words "There was no room at the inn." Raising his arms, they fold down then close.

Fruitcake, poinsettias, fudge fill our parsonage, cookies, cards, and packages for the minister and his family.

His daughter's presents are not wrapped. Red tissue paper rustles, their shadows argue against the wall his voice commanding, "Hurry up." He's naked swilling clear vodka. Sobbing she cries, "You'll wake her."

Silent night Holy night All is calm All is bright.

I will stay here in this closet until morning when they call me to open my presents

all the tags in her handwriting.

—Joan

Emotional Legacies

While depression is common to many raised with addiction, depression and anxiety disorders are more common with the additional experience of physical and/or sexual abuse. A generalized anxiety disorder is marked by unrealistic worry, apprehension, and uncertainty. Depending on the symptoms, posttraumatic stress disorder (PTSD), panic attacks, and phobias are subsets of the psychiatric category of anxiety disorder.

Janet was ultimately treated for both depression and anxiety after her second divorce from two long-term marriages to addicts. Until the divorce, she had not reached out for help and by the time she sought it she was experiencing a major depression. She was experiencing slurred speech, the inability to make decisions, extremely poor self-care, diminished expectations, etc. The depression was treated with antidepressants. What then became obvious was a long-standing anxiety disorder. She fretted and worried about every minor and major detail in her life. Everything in life was a potential problem. To ask basic questions of someone in a store would send her into an emotional panic. Janet was raised in a physically threatening, alcoholic home and experienced sexual abuse for a period of two years by two perpetrators who were friends of her parents.

Thomas started experiencing panic attacks shortly after he began recovery from his compulsive overeating. He was raised in an alcoholic family with a schizophrenic mother who subjected him to extremely cruel physical punishments. Food had always been his medicator. Without the sugar, and without any recovery from the emotional pain in his life, his fears quickly rose to the surface and he was hospitalized three times for what would ultimately be diagnosed as panic attacks (characterized by intense anxiety, often a feeling of impending death, heart palpitations, shortness of breath, and sweating.)

Having been the victim of physical or sexual abuse strongly contributes to the likelihood of experiencing PTSD as well.

Karen was raised in a battering, alcoholic family. Between the ages of seven and twelve, she was also sexually abused by her older brother. She has chronically suffered from PTSD. At the age of thirty-six, she is self-supporting but lives her life quite isolated. She is hypervigilant to the first sign of danger, physical and emotional. She perceives danger when she feels misunderstood, not agreed with—limiting her social world considerably. She has been in the same job fifteen years, not wanting any advancement or change, liking the security. She is far too frightened of intimacy to allow herself a close and loving relationship. She lies awake at night, listening to noises, or frequently wakes up in the night, startled and unsure of her safety. From the outside, she simply looks like someone more introverted and content to live her life this way. All the while, she is simply trying to contain her fears.

For Karen, her entire life is structured by her need to create safety in response to her PTSD. For others, there may be only one or two symptoms of PTSD. Sondra has been a responsible adult child, a superachiever in her young adult life. But at the age of twenty-seven, as she was traveling for her company, she found herself having nightmares that woke her from a sound sleep. She began to relive the violence that she was raised with. It was as if she were eight years old again. She didn't talk about it or do anything about it. It was only when she was in couples' counseling that her husband leaked this secret. That is when her recovery had the chance to begin.

Stereotypically, when we think of trauma we think of public, catastrophic events that can overwhelm an adult. But what distinguishes childhood trauma from occurrences like combat stress is simply that the injuries occur to children. "Be kind to me, Lord," reads the epigram for the National Children's Defense Fund, "My boat is so small and the sea is so wide." A child's personality and neurology—the little boat he or she must navigate in—are still developing. Because they are chronic when raised with addiction, childhood injuries—even when mild by some people's experiences—can have long-lasting effects because they occur while the very structures of the body, brain, and personality are being formed.

These are stressed children; they have a harder time modulating feelings and negotiating conflict than other children. They are much more prone to addictive disorders. While for some, the anxiety, panic, depression, or addictive disorders may begin in their adolescent years, for others these problems occur in adulthood. While a trauma survivor may no longer be subject to abuse, he or she may not have found a therapeutic avenue in which to resolve the pain. Victims often try to cope by self-administering substances, such as alcohol, cocaine, amphetamines, heroin, or even food, to quiet the pain. Often their use of a medicating substance or high-risk behavior is in response to the anxiety disorder or depression. In working with addiction, it is becoming clear, the more abused you were as a child, the more addictions you are likely to have.

Undoing Denial

Today many marriage and family therapists, social workers, and psychologists work with adults who were molested as children. Many adult victims find solace and understanding by joining a self-help or support group comprised of other adult victims. The validation that occurs within a group setting profoundly reduces the shame experienced by the survivor. The issues of Not Talking, Not Trusting, and Not Feeling need to be discovered and shared. Many books have been written for both men and women who are survivors of abuse. No one should have to continue to live with the shame and secrecy of what happened to them and the many consequences of that experience.

It is truth that will lead to recovery. It is denial that keeps us shamebound. This in turn creates or perpetuates unhealthy relationships, compulsive behavior, and/or addictions. It is shame that keeps us immobilized and depressed. Although we were victimized as children, we do not deserve to continue to live our lives as victims.

As traumatic as the experiences were, we survived. *We are survivors.* It is important to allow ourselves to remember the past so we can separate ourselves from the abuser and the internalized shame. We need to talk about the experiences so that we can put them into perspective. In childhood we saw these events through the eyes of a vulnerable child. This child believed that we must have deserved what we got, that we were bad. As an adult, it is safer to speak to the injustice and the unfairness and the terror that were part of the experiences. It is important to receive validation for our experiences. We deserve to know that our perceptions were correct. Not talking about it is a form of minimizing and denying, a way of continuing to negate and deny ourselves. Truth is the only way out of the cycle of abuse.

Anger

Anger is part of the healing process. Victims and survivors are either totally detached from, extremely frightened of, or overwhelmed by this feeling. If you don't feel anger, ask yourself, "Where did it go? Why isn't it safe?" Be open to the fact that anger does exist. It is there. It just may not be very visible. People may need to confront their rage before they can separate out anger and any other feelings. People who are abused and unable to focus their rage at the abuser, take their rage elsewhere. It can become an addiction or show up as compulsive behavior such as perfectionism, workaholism, critical self-talk, chronic illness, compulsive masturbation, eating disorders, or self-mutilation. This is rage turned inward, an act of personal violence.

It is okay to be angry. It is not okay to be violent with oneself or others.

There are constructive ways to own and release anger. This is best done in a therapeutic context. There are many well-trained people working with people who come from battering or sexually abusive histories. Recognizing and challenging the anger constructively will allow you to identify your needs. Anger will help you identify limits and boundaries you need to set. When owned and expressed constructively, it will give you the courage to be self-caring.

You are no longer the victimized child. You are an adult who was once abused. You can go back and retrieve the power you didn't have then by challenging the internalized messages that you learned to believe. You will garner power in recovery as you learn to establish healthy boundaries. By establishing boundaries and setting limits, you will begin to find the freedom of using the words "No" and "Yes." It was not safe to say "No" as a child. Without the freedom to say "No," "Yes" was said with tremendous fear and helplessness or out of a desperate need for approval and love.

Recovery means talking about the many times you couldn't say No but wanted to, and the anger and pain that goes with that. Recovery means recognizing the ability to say No as a friend to protect you. You have the power and right to say No and Yes. You will find that Yes is a gift that is offered freely rather than out of fear or the need for approval. Recognize that by saying No, you are actually saying Yes to yourself.

"As I was growing up, I remember really wanting only one thing—to be able to do it differently than I saw it being done around me. So, when, two days before my twenty-third birthday, my husband was put in jail for a felony DUI, I looked into the passive eyes of my child, whom I had just thrown across the room, and felt my world and my sanity crumble. I was doing it just the same way they had done.

Two days later, I was in therapy with a psychologist who introduced me to Al-Anon and within the year I began to learn to do it differently. For the first time in my life, I began to see I had a choice. What a miraculous concept. I was building myself into a whole person even though my husband's alcoholism progressed rapidly for the next six years.

My husband has now had five years of sobriety. We learned this is a family illness and there can be family recovery if at least one family member tries to find alternatives. I am finally doing it differently, and for me, it is a better way. At last, finally, I had a choice."

Chapter 7

The Adult Child

Children raised with addiction move into adulthood with incredible strengths as a result of survivorship. They pat themselves on the back and don't want to look behind. In time they begin to experience problems as a result of:

- the inability —to trust their own perception
  —to trust others
  —to identify needs
  —to identify feelings
  —to listen
  —to relax
  —to initiate
- fear —of feelings
  —of conflict
  —of rejection or abandonment
- the need to control to feel safe or ward off shame
- impoverished expectations
- unrealistic expectations
- rage
- depression
- substance abuse
- sex addiction
- work addiction
- love and relationship difficulty
- pathological gambling
- compulsive spending
- eating disorders
- repetitive addictive relationships

One asks, "Who isn't affected by these issues?" To some degree we can all be. But the phrase "some degree" is important here. Adult children experience these difficulties to an extreme. The difficulties interfere with the ability to genuinely discover happiness and meaningfulness in life. It is my belief that we as adult children deserve more than the ability to survive. It is my hope that this book offers choices about how to live our lives.

Recovery begins with accepting two basic rights:

1. We have the right to talk about the real issues.
2. We have the right to feel.

Judith Viorst wrote in *Necessary Losses,* "It is true that as long as we live we may keep repeating the patterns established in childhood. It is true that the present is powerfully shaped by the past. But it is also true that insight at any age keeps us from singing the same sad songs again."

To be able to put the past behind and not repeat those same sad songs, adult children need to take four primary steps.

1. Explore Past History

Recovery begins with speaking our truth, naming our reality, our experiences. One does not explore the past to assign blame but to discover and acknowledge reality. It is my belief that family members truly want the best for each other and that begins with honesty. We aren't betraying our parents or siblings when we become honest about our reality. If there is an act of betrayal, it is with the addiction, the dysfunction of the family system. When we do not talk honestly about our experiences we ultimately betray ourselves and the potential health of the family.

Exploring past history means asking questions such as "What happened that was hurtful to me?" and "What didn't I have that I needed?"

To let go of the past we must be willing to break through denial so we can grieve our pain. In other words, we have to admit to ourselves the truth of what happened, rather than hide or keep secret the hurt and wounds that occurred. It is difficult to speak honestly today when we have had to deny, minimize, or discount the first fifteen or twenty years of our lives. There is no doubt denial became a skill that served us as a child in a survival mode. Unfortunately denial, which begins as a defense, becomes a skill that interferes with how we live our life today. We take the skill of minimizing, rationalizing, discounting into every aspect of our life. When we let go of denial and acknowledge the past, it gives us the opportunity to identify our losses and to grieve the pain associated. It is the opportunity to genuinely put the past behind us. Exploring the past is an act of empowerment.

It is vital, however, that we go beyond the first step. Otherwise, the grief process simply becomes a blaming process. That has never been the intent of adult child recovery, nor should it be.

We continue with recovery as we move from the process of breaking our denial and grieving our pain.

2. Connect the Past to the Present

Connect the past to the present means asking, "How does this past pain and loss influence who I am today? How does the past affect who I am as a parent, in the workplace, in a relationship, how I feel about myself?" The cause-and-effect connections we discover between our past losses and present lives give us a sense of direction. It allows us to become more centered in the here and now. This clarity will identify the areas we need to work on.

3. Challenge Internalized Beliefs

Challenging internalized beliefs means asking, "What beliefs have I internalized from my growing-up years? Are they helpful or hurtful to me today? What beliefs would support me in living a healthier life?" So often we internalized beliefs such as "It is not okay to say no" or "Other people's needs are more important than my own"; "No one will listen to what I have to say" or "The world owes me and I am entitled"; and "People will take advantage of you every chance they can." If these beliefs are getting in the way of how we want to live our lives, we need to take responsibility for what we do with them. We need to let them go and recreate new beliefs in their place.

4. Learn New Skills

Learning new skills means asking, "What did I not learn that would help me today?" As well, many skills we learned prematurely and were developed from a basis of fear and shame. When that occurs there is a tendency to feel like an imposter. In those situations, addressing the feelings and beliefs associated with the skill will make it more likely we can feel greater confidence in those skills.

With the many different issues we may need to address—from healthier decision making to realistic expectations, setting limits to expressing feelings—these four steps are not always linear. In general, we do them in the order listed, but as you will quickly experience, you often keep coming back to a previous step to do another piece of work.

The knowledge that comes in owning our past and connecting it to the present is vital in developing empathy for the strength of both our defenses and skills. It also helps us to lessen our shame and not hold ourselves accountable for the pain we have carried. When we understand there are reasons for why we have lived our lives as we have, and that it is not because there is something inherently wrong with who we are, that we are not bad, the understanding fuels our ongoing healing. The change we want to create in our life will be made directly as a result of letting go of old, hurtful belief systems and learning new skills.

Addressing adult child issues is about taking responsibility for what we do with our lives. It allows us to live with honesty and choices. We no longer have to pretend things are different than how they are.

Family Tree

To better understand your family system, it is often helpful to have a mental picture of your family. To the best of your ability, fill in the names of your family members. For many people this exercise reminds them of how little they know of their family history. If you can't complete many of the names, simply acknowledge the fact there are missing pieces to your history. What does that mean or imply to you? You may choose to seek out others to assist you in filling in the blanks.

Indicate with a circle (○) the names of people whom you know have experienced alcohol and other drug problems.

Check (✓) the names of people whom you know have experienced eating disorder problems.

Mark with an "X" the names of people whom you know were physical abusers and/or were abused.

Indicate with a square symbol (□) the names of people whom you know were incest perpetrators and/or incest victims.

Indicate with a star (★) the names of people whom you know experienced other identifiable dysfunctions, and name the problem.

Indicate by circling the names of people whom you have held a strong positive regard for. When you are done, do some writing as to why you feel the positive attachment.

MOTHER'S SIDE

Maternal Grandparents
Grandmother/Grandfather

______ ______

Name aunts with spouses

______ ______

Name children

______
______
______
______
______ ______
______
______
______
______

Name uncles with spouses

______ ______

Name children

______
______
______
______
______ ______
______
______
______
______

FATHER'S SIDE

Paternal Grandparents
Grandmother/Grandfather

______ ______

Name aunts with spouses

______ ______

Name children

______
______
______
______
______ ______
______
______
______
______

Name uncles with spouses

______ ______

Name children

______
______
______
______
______ ______
______
______
______
______

PARENTS

2nd Husband (Stepfather)	MOM	DAD	2nd Wife (Stepmother)

Sisters & Brothers (include yourself)	Spouse	Children	

Talking

One of the consequences of growing up in a home with the Don't Talk rule is that people develop a silent tolerance for inconsistencies, untruths, and painful feelings. Reflect on people you may have talked to about problems at home when you were a young child and teenager. Check the frequency with which you can remember talking about problems to your:

FREQUENCY OF TALKING ABOUT PROBLEMS

	Never	Once	Occasionally	Often
Mother ______________	☐	☐	☐	☐
Father ______________	☐	☐	☐	☐
Stepmother ______________	☐	☐	☐	☐
Stepfather ______________	☐	☐	☐	☐
Brother ______________	☐	☐	☐	☐
Brother ______________	☐	☐	☐	☐
Sister ______________	☐	☐	☐	☐
Sister ______________	☐	☐	☐	☐
Grandparents ______________	☐	☐	☐	☐
Other family members ______________	☐	☐	☐	☐
Teacher ______________	☐	☐	☐	☐
Counselor ______________	☐	☐	☐	☐
Clergy ______________	☐	☐	☐	☐
Friend ______________	☐	☐	☐	☐
Neighbor ______________	☐	☐	☐	☐
Other ______________	☐	☐	☐	☐

List the people in your life today whom you are willing to share your problems with:

____

____

____

____

In some instances, certain issues were present in your family life as a child and a teenager that may have prevented you from talking about problematic areas of your life. Circle those that were true for you:

- I felt ashamed
- I felt disloyal, as if I were betraying
- I was embarrassed
- I didn't understand what was occurring well enough to talk about it
- I was afraid I wouldn't be believed
- I was specifically instructed not to talk
- It was insinuated in nonverbal ways that I should not talk
- It seemed as though no one else was talking
- I believed something bad would happen if I talked
- I came to believe that nothing good would have come from talking

If as an adult, you still have difficulty talking about your childhood and adolescence, put a check (✔) by the above statement(s) that apply to you today.

List the people in your life today with whom you already are or are willing to talk to about your childhood:

____

____

____

If you:

- feel a sense of shame when talking about your growing-up years, try to understand that you weren't at fault—your parents would have liked it to have been different.
- feel a sense of guilt when talking, trust that you are not betraying

your parents, your family, or yourself. If there is any betrayal, you are betraying the addictive system.

- feel a sense of confusion about your childhood, that's probably an accurate description of how life has been for you—confusing. When attempting to explain irrational behavior in a rational manner, it will sound confusing. Talk—it will help you develop greater clarity.
- fear that you will not be believed, a great deal of information is available which will substantiate that your experiences are not unique. (Refer to the appendices.)
- have been instructed (specifically or nonverbally) not to talk, recognize that instruction was motivated by fear or guilt. You don't have to live that way any longer.
- have experienced something negative from people you spoke with in the past, you are now free to choose a healthier support system.
- have been conditioned to believe that "nothing good comes from talking," put faith in the belief it is only when you finally begin to speak your truth that you will be able to put the past behind and experience the joy of the present.

Talk about your childhood.

Now ask yourself, "What are the areas of my life I hesitate to tell others about and what are the beliefs that get in the way?"

Denial

In recognizing each family member's denial, it is possible to see how the whole family environment has been affected. Think about times your family discounted or minimized situations or feelings:

I can remember the time (Mom): minimized
discounted
rationalized

____

____

____

____

I can remember the time (Dad): minimized / discounted / rationalized

____
____
____
____

I can remember the time (Stepparent): minimized / discounted / rationalized

____
____
____
____

I can remember the time (Brother): minimized / discounted / rationalized

____
____
____
____

I can remember the time (Sister): minimized / discounted / rationalized

____
____
____
____

Now, reflect on your adulthood, complete the following:
Today I minimize (rationalize or discount)

1. ____
____
____

when in reality . . .

____
____
____

Today I minimize (rationalize or discount)

2. ____
____
____

when in reality . . .

____
____
____

Today I minimize (rationalize or discount)

3. ____
____
____

when in reality . . .

____
____
____

Today I minimize (rationalize or discount)

4. ____
____
____

when in reality . . .

____

____

____

As you work through these exercises, you'll begin to recognize yourself in the act of denial. As a result, this awareness will allow you to be more honest, to better identify your own feelings, and eventually to identify your needs and offer the opportunity for greater self-care. Eliminating denial will allow you to see things for what they are, which will alleviate long-range problems and allow you to begin to live in the "here and now."

Feelings

Our negative feelings are more likely to lessen when we are able to talk about them. When we don't express these feelings they accumulate. Years ago, as small children, we began rolling our feelings up in a bundle like a small piece of snow rolling down a hill and these feelings have now become a giant snowball. By the time the snowball reaches the bottom of the hill—by the time we have grown up—the feelings have simply been stored up, painful feelings upon painful feelings. No wonder we are scared. Now, when we do get in touch with all of our feelings, we are understandably overwhelmed.

Present-day disappointments, losses, angers, and fears become intertwined with the old disappointments, losses, angers, and fears, making it difficult to separate the old issues from the new ones. Having a feeling does not mean you need to act on it. How one feels and what one does with those feelings are separate issues. In early recovery, being aware of your feelings and identifying them is significant. Let your feelings be your friend, not something to be denied or minimized. Feelings are not there to rule you, but to be cues and signals to tell you something. Acceptance of feelings, combined with the ability to express them, will decrease fear and generate greater inner confidence. Feelings seem inappropriate only when they are not understood.

What are the messages that interfere with your willingness to show specific feelings?

Where did you get these messages?

What is the price you pay for maintaining these messages?

If you are inexperienced at owning your feelings, it will be important for you to know the value of being able to identify and express them. Some benefits are:

- When I know my feelings and am more honest with myself, then I have the option of being more honest with others.
- When I am in touch with my feelings, I will be in a better position to be close to other people.
- When I know how I feel, I can begin to ask for what I need.
- When I am able to experience feelings, I feel more alive.

Identify two more reasons that it is of value to be able to identify and express feelings.

From the list below, circle the feelings with which you identify.

love
fear
worry
sadness
discouragement
anger
hurt
jealousy
shame
happiness
guilt
confusion
frustration
loneliness
embarrassment
hate

List in written form when and where you experience these feelings. If the identification of feelings is difficult, make copies of this page and on a daily or weekly basis acknowledge to yourself what feelings you have been experiencing. Try to share these with another person. The more specific you can be about your feelings, the more you can understand and accept them, and the more apt you are to be able to do something constructive about them. While positive feelings are the ones people seek, negative feelings can be viewed as cues or signals that can give information about what is needed.

"When I feel sad, it may possibly mean I need support."
"When I am angry, I probably need to clarify my stance."
"When I am scared, I need to let someone else know that."

By viewing the more painful feelings as signals, it is easier to accept them and to utilize them constructively. By identifying feelings one is less apt to be overwhelmed by emotion and end up depressed, confused, or enraged.

With the following exercise you can gain insight into and awareness of family patterns. On a scale of one to five—one being the least often expressed, five being the most often expressed—rate your parents' frequency of expression.

FEELINGS	Mother	Father	FEELINGS	Mother	Father
Love	12345	12345	Shame	12345	12345
Fear	12345	12345	Happiness	12345	12345
Worry	12345	12345	Guilt	12345	12345
Sadness	12345	12345	Confusion	12345	12345
Discouragement	12345	12345	Frustration	12345	12345
Anger	12345	12345	Loneliness	12345	12345
Hurt	12345	12345	Embarrassment	12345	12345
Jealousy	12345	12345	Hate	12345	12345

You can also ask yourself which feelings you wanted expressed more often, and which ones less.

Can you see any repetitive patterns for you in adulthood?

Crying

As a child you may have learned not to cry, or to cry silently alone. Thirty-six-year-old Jerry, a recovering addict, was talking about the issue of crying. He said he was the child who never cried. When he was very young, he remembered crying only once, and that was when a pet died. He entered adolescence and adulthood being "tough" and "surviving." Jerry told his counselor about his complete inability to shed tears over any of his personal misfortunes, which included nine hospitalizations for alcoholism. Surrender is essential for an addict's recovery. It includes the breaking of the denial system about one's situation in life, mentally, emotionally, physically, and spiritually. Jerry's surrender began when the tears started to flow the day he was admitted to his tenth treatment program. Jerry needed to cry—he needed to quit being "tough," "alone," and in the denial trap of not talking, not feeling, and not trusting. The tears were the breakthrough. If you are an adult child who can identify with patterns of not crying, or crying alone and silently, you must understand the necessity of breaking the pattern before you will be able to affect your own recovery process. This surrender is the first step in recovery.

While many adult children follow the aforementioned pattern, there are those who find themselves crying, yet not understanding the reason for the tears. Some find they cry at inappropriate times, while others find they cry at the appropriate times, but there is an overabundance of tears. Cheryl, thirty-five, says, "I'm so tired of crying. I never cried as a child, and today I cry at the least little thing. I cry if I get scared, I cry if I feel rejected, I cry if I hear a sad story on the news, I cry when I read a nice, warm story in the paper. I don't seem to have any control. It's really embarrassing, but more than anything, it really scares me."

It is important to 1) recognize the need to cry, 2) give yourself permission to cry, 3) let another person know about this, and 4) let that other person be available to be supportive of you.

You will need to reevaluate the messages you previously received about crying, such as "It doesn't do any good to cry"; "Boys don't cry"; "Only sissies cry"; "I'll smack you harder if you cry." New messages need to be "It's okay if I cry"; "It's important that I allow myself to cry"; "It's a healthy release"; "I'll probably feel better."

As a child what did you do with your tears?

- Did you cry?
- Did others know when you were crying?
- Did you let others comfort you when you were crying?
- What did you do to prevent yourself from crying?

Now ask yourself:

- When do you cry?

- Do you ever cry?
- Do you only cry when alone?
- Do you cry hard, or do you cry slowly and silently?
- Do you cry because people hurt your feelings?
- Do you cry for no apparent reason?
- Do others know when you cry?
- Do others see you cry?
- Do others hear you cry?
- Do you let others comfort you when you cry?
- Do you let others hold you?
- Do you let them just sit with you?
- What do you do to prevent yourself from crying?
- Do you tell yourself you are stupid for letting another person hurt your feelings?
- Do you get angry with yourself for crying?
- How is your pattern as an adult different from that of a child?

Read through these questions again, slowly, and then share what you know about yourself with another person. Choose a person with whom you feel safe—a therapist, an Al-Anon member, a sponsor, a friend—someone with whom you feel you can allow yourself to be vulnerable. Remember, others may have old messages about the stigma of crying, too, and might welcome the opportunity to talk about an issue many people never take the time to explore.

You may also need to think about the basis of your fear of crying. For the supercontrolling person, fear of crying usually means a fear of falling apart. It is a fear of losing control; the fear that once crying starts, it will lead to hysterical behavior or that you will be unable to stop. The greater your fear, the greater the need to let others offer support. Recognize the need to establish a situation that is both protective and healthy. While crying may feel very frightening, you do not need to fear you will go into hysteria. You may cry for five minutes, even ten minutes. As a therapist, I have seen hundreds of people cry, and they never needed to be carted away! Remember, you have accumulated a great deal of unresolved feelings. Your tears are usually related to sorrow, confusion, loneliness, and loss.

Fear

You may experience an overwhelming sense of fear. Much of the time that fear is unidentifiable. These fearful times are often episodic, periods of extreme fearfulness contrasted by periods totally devoid of fear. On the other hand, you may find yourself existing in a perpetual state of unidentifiable fear.

Many people are fearful of expressing their needs, fearing a loss of love should they express a want. Dawn said, "I've grown a lot, but I still feel gut-level fear when I express my wants and needs to my husband. It's difficult to be spontaneously open and self-disclosing. I'm afraid he won't love me."

As you move from childhood to adulthood, you may continue to experience fear of confrontation. For many, confrontation is a simple disagreement or questioning. Nonetheless, the fear is intense and based on what they perceive to be a real confrontation. These fears may stem from years of a parent's harassment, which always resulted in feeling guilty or humiliated. These fears persist because there was never any constructive or healthy disagreement within the family. Any expressed disagreement resulted in yelling and loud arguing because the addict could not tolerate anyone disagreeing with him/her. Disagreement was perceived as betrayal and resulted in actions that belittled and condemned the child.

when I think about my Dad drinking again I get shakey inside

I feel scared about things and worry most when everything is OK. I feel tied up and can't let go. I want to untie the Knots and be free.

Janice, 44

Adult children who during their growing-up years experienced a lot of fear of the unknown, never knowing what to expect next, will continue to experience uncertainty and fear of the unknown. The fear of the unknown can keep one immobilized, and being stuck in fear, itself, immobilizes one emotionally. It will result in a tendency to discount one's own perceptions and not have the courage to check out other people's perceptions. The results are isolation, low self-esteem, and frequently depression and anxiety. (Should you believe your life is negatively impacted by a chronic state of fear or worry, or a chronic state of joylessness or panic attacks, consult a physician immediately.)

Answer the following questions:

- What did you fear as a child?
- Did you fear you were going to be left alone?
- Were you afraid you were going to get hit?
- Were you afraid your mom or your dad did not love you?
- What did you do when you were fearful as a child?
- Did you go to your room and cry?
- Did you get angry instead?
- Did you hide in a closet?
- Did you ask a brother or sister to come and be with you?
- Did others know that you were afraid?
- Do you think your mom knew?
- Do you think your sister or your grandparents possibly knew?
- How did you express this fear?
- Did you wet the bed?
- Did you mask your fear with anger?
- How is that pattern similar in your adulthood?
- Do you still go off by yourself when afraid?
- Do you still get angry instead?
- Are you sharing your fears with someone, or are you still pretending you're not afraid?

Ask those questions of another adult, someone you trust, and share your answers with one another.

A goal in recovery is not to feel "less than" or be immobilized in fear. Fear can be a wonderful motivator and certainly a cue to what we may need.

Anger

Today our criminal justice system is inundated with angry, substance-abusing offenders. On any given day, some 1.7 million men and women are incarcerated in federal and state prisons and local jails in the United States, and a recent study suggests that more than 80 percent of them are involved in substance use. Another way of viewing this is that one in every 144 American adults is behind bars for a crime in which substances are involved.

The feeling of anger is natural to everyone, but when you are raised with addiction, anger is often repressed, twisted and distorted. It is a feeling that is invariably denied yet manifests itself in a multitude of ways—depressive behavior, overeating, oversleeping, placating, and psychosomatic problems. Most likely you experienced living with chronic anger or rage, or an always-simmering low level of anger or anger avoidance. One parent operated on one extreme, while the other was at the other extreme. Anger is often expressed through a tense silence, through mutual blaming, or through one-sided blaming coupled with one-sided acceptance. Today we repeat that pattern. We repeat the extreme behaviors and often choose a mate to parallel our pattern.

Lee, age thirty-one, was aware of his anger but didn't find outlets for expression. "I have needed to let go of the bitterness and hatred. I see I have denied myself so much. I have not let myself get close to anybody, men or women. I have allowed myself to be eaten up inside. Oh, I looked okay to the world, and have done okay in my work, but I can't let anyone get close enough to me or they would see this ugliness."

Carrie described the consequence to her fear of any conflict erupting into violence. "After four years of marriage in which there were very few arguments, I woke my husband one morning and said, 'I'm leaving now,' and smiled." She said there had been no discussion of her wanting out of the marriage or her wanting anything to be different. She said she wasn't angry, she simply wanted out. She explained she had never been allowed to argue about anything as a child, and when her husband raised his voice, she'd simply agree to his wants. She walked out of a marriage that possibly could have been saved had she had the ability simply to disagree, had she had the ability to express what it was she needed or wanted. But for her, the fear of dealing with anger, either her own or her husband's, was too great to risk.

While some adult children are anger avoidant and many others chronically angry or simply bitter about life, all have a definite need to resolve issues. While anger is a natural human emotion, what you do with anger is learned and can be reshaped to better meet your own needs. Remember, feelings are a natural part of you, use them as signals to help direct you.

Now ask yourself:

- What did you do with your anger as a child?
- Did you swallow and not become aware of it?
- Did you play the piano extra hard?
- Did you hit your brothers and sisters?
- Did you go to your room and cry?
- What did other family members do with their anger?
- Did your dad just drink more?
- Did your mom just drink more?
- Did your brother just shrug his shoulders and go outside and play with his friends?
- Did your sister just cry silently?
- Are you afraid you will go into a rage?
- Are you afraid you will start crying to the point of becoming hysterical?
- Is there a fear about what would happen if you really acknowledged your anger today?

Talk with others about their anger. Ask them what they get angry about. Ask them how they express their anger. Compare patterns. You'll find out you are not alone.

Make a list of all the things you could have been angry about as a child. Example:

- I could have been angry with my dad for hitting my mom when she was drunk.
- I could have been angry with my dad for giving my dog away.
- I could have been angry with my mom the time she passed out on Christmas Eve.

- I could have been angry with my mom for not listening to me when I told her dad was drunk.

Now, make a list of things that as an adult you could be angry about but aren't.

Example:

- I could be angry with my dad for never getting sober.
- I could be angry with my sister for never going to see my mom.
- I could be angry with my husband for not being more willing to listen to me when I want to talk about my mom or dad.
- I could be angry when I think people have taken advantage of me.

When you have approximately four or five examples of situations in which you could be angry as a child or adult, draw a large "X" across the words "I could have been" and "I could be" in every one of those sentences. Then write, "I am," "I was," or "I am still," depending on whether or not you are still angry.

Example:

- I am still angry with my dad for hitting my mom when she was drunk.
- I am angry with my dad for never getting sober.
- I am still angry with my dad for giving my dog away.
- I was angry with my mom the time she passed out on Christmas Eve.
- I am angry when I think people have taken advantage of me.
- I am still angry with my mom for not listening to me when I told her dad was drunk.
- I am angry with my husband for not being more willing to listen to me when I want to talk about my mom or dad.

Now, reflect on those sentences and thoughts—be aware of how you feel.

If you are working on this exercise with someone, tell him or her how you feel. Is it difficult to admit your feelings? Some of you will find relief in simply acknowledging past pain. Others won't like the feelings at all. Remember, acknowledging anger, as well as other feelings, is a necessary part of the recovery, and the more you share your experiences with yourself and with others, the more comfortable recovery will be for you. A secondary benefit is an increased closeness and bond with those friends with whom you choose to share your feelings.

Guilt

Imagine holding on to guilt for ten, thirty, possibly as many as sixty years, especially guilt about something over which one has absolutely no control. When children are constantly made to feel guilty, they invariably continue adding more and more guilt to their inner selves as they grow up.

I met Jake when he was seventy-four years old. He came to me asking if I would participate in a task force for a local helping agency. After he had introduced himself and told me about the needs of the agency, he admitted he was not familiar with my work but had been told by others that I worked with "kids whose parents are alcoholics."

I acknowledged the information he had been given was correct, and I began explaining the nature of what I do. I had been speaking for only about three to four minutes when he interrupted me suddenly, saying, "Yeah . . . yeah . . . my dad was alcoholic. Uh, he died." His gaze dropped from my eyes, and he began looking fixedly at the floor. "Yeah," he said. "I was thirteen." His gaze turned to the ceiling. "He was thirty-one or thirty-two, I guess. Died in an accident. He was drunk when it happened." Haltingly, he continued, "You know, I never understood. I never understood. You know I tried to be good. I never knew what he wanted though. I know I did things he didn't like, but I wasn't a bad kid."

Jake had carried his guilt for sixty-one years. He was not rambling in semisenility, he was feeling pure guilt. He still believed he was responsible for his father's drinking and, ultimately, his father's death. He had carried all these years of guilt because he had no understanding of the disease process.

James told me, "I have carried guilt feelings throughout my life because I didn't want the responsibility of raising my brother and sisters. I deserted my mom when I was eighteen and joined the army. I deserted her—just like my alcoholic father."

For one and a half years in Al-Anon, Julie, age thirty-five, has been seriously addressing her issues around guilt. "I have a lot of issues to deal with about my mother—her constant criticism, guilt because I didn't know why I was being criticized, and finally, my guilt for being alive."

People need to reassess those things for which they held themselves responsible. The Serenity Prayer, which is the hallmark philosophy of Alcoholics Anonymous and Al-Anon, says,

God grant me the serenity
To accept the things I cannot change,
The courage to change the things I can,
And the wisdom to know the difference.

The more you understand, the easier it is to accept that you aren't responsible for your parents' addiction or their behaviors. It is important you realize that as a young child you had only emotional, psychological, and physical capabilities to behave as just that—a child. Once you have accepted that, it is easier not to be so self-blaming and guilt ridden.

Think about the guilt you still carry. Do you ever say, "If only I had . . . "? Take some time right now to examine your guilt feelings by working the following exercise.

As a child, if only I had . . .
As a teenager, if only I had . . .

Now, seriously answer, would have any other six-year-old, twelve-year-old, or eighteen-year-old in the same situation, with the same circumstances, behaved any differently? In fact, even as a twenty-five-year-old, or a thirty-five-year-old, without knowledge of addiction and its many ramifications, would it be possible to respond differently? As an adult, the tendency to accept all guilt is a pattern that needs to be broken.

Now, ask yourself:

- What did I do with my guilt as a child?
- Was I forever apologizing?
- Was I a perfect child making up for what I thought I was doing wrong?
- Was I an angry child?

It is important to gain a realistic perspective of situations that you have the power to affect. We often have a distorted perception of where our power lies and as a result live with much false guilt. True guilt is remorse or regret we feel for something we have done or not done. False guilt is taking on the feeling for someone else's behavior and actions.

Because this is usually a lifelong habit, it is important to go back and delineate historically what you were and were not responsible for. That will assist us in being more skilled in recognizing our lifelong pattern of taking on false guilt and stopping it.

Rewrite the following sentence stems and fill in the blanks. Write "No," in the first blank, and then continue by finishing the sentence:

____ I was not responsible for ________________________________
when he/she did ____
____
it wasn't my fault when ___________________________________
____
it wasn't my duty or obligation to ____________________________
____

Then take the time to write about anything else you might feel guilty about that wasn't your fault.

When people feel guilty, many times they end up crying, looking as if they are sad or disappointed, or twisting the guilt into anger. Disguising one's true feelings by putting up a false front is a common practice. Out of the need to survive, people will create distorted expressions of feelings.

What do you feel guilty about?

- Little things in everyday life
- Everything in everyday life

What do you do when you feel guilty?

- Buy presents for the person toward whom you feel the guilt
- Get depressed
- Get angry
- Berate yourself

When you are feeling guilt, a simple exercise is to ask yourself:

- What did I do to affect the situation?
- What can I do to make it any different?
- Can I accept that I did all that I was able to do with the resources available?

Give yourself permission to make mistakes. Take responsibility for what is yours, but don't accept responsibility for what is not yours. You will need to work on your self-image and your ability to understand and express your own fear and anger, as well as to learn ways to deal with your guilt.

The possibilities for masking feelings are many. Anxiety, depression, overeating, insomnia, oversleeping, high blood pressure, overwork, always being sick, always being tired, being overly nice—the list goes on. These consequences affect not only your life, but they will interfere with your relationships with others—your spouse, your lover, your children, your friends. Now is the time to change the pattern, but please don't try to do it in a vacuum. Let others be a part of this new growth.

Recovery is the ability to tolerate feelings
without the need to medicate.

Daughters of the Bottle

until i was twenty-two
i didn't think anyone else had a drunk for a mother
then i met lori joannie and susan
i recognized them immediately by their stay away smiles
they were leaders in their work
competent imposters like me
who would say they were sorry
if somebody bumped into them on a crowded street
i call on them once in a while
they always come
children of alcoholics always do.

—Jane

Reshaping Roles

Responsible Child

The responsible child, otherwise known as the "nine-year-old going on thirty-five," has probably come to find himself as very organized and goal oriented. The responsible child is adept at planning and manipulating others to get things accomplished, allowing him to be in a leadership position. He is often independent and self-reliant, capable of accomplishments and achievements. But because these accomplishments are made less out of choice and more out of a necessity to survive (emotionally, if not physically), there is usually a price paid for this "early maturity."

For example: "As a result of being the 'little adult' in my house, I didn't have time to play baseball because I had to make dinner for my sisters."

Complete the following:

As a result of being the "little adult" in my house, I didn't have time to ________________________________
because ________________________________
____

As a result of being the "little adult" in my house, I didn't have time to ________________________________
because ________________________________
____

As a result of being the "little adult" in my house, I didn't have time to ________________________________
because ________________________________
____

As a result of being the "little adult" in my house, I didn't have time to ________________________________
because ________________________________
____

For the person who has the ability to accomplish a great deal, the issue of control often creates problem areas in adult life. Accompanying a strong need to be in control is an extreme fear of being totally out of control, particularly with feelings. As Sue said, "If I permitted myself to throw one plate out of frustration, there would be nothing stopping me from throwing thirty!"

Because so much of our life has been lived in extremes, we feel as if we are "in control" or "out of control." We don't know about "some" control. We view it as impossible as being "a little bit pregnant." Perceiving control to be an all-or-nothing experience, we don't want to give it up. We don't want to give it up because it once protected us. Giving up control is frightening because it has been vital to our safety. Control of the external forces in the environment is a survival mechanism. It may be self-protection in a physical sense. It may be what allowed you to make sense out of your life. Controlling behavior was an attempt to bring order and consistency into inconsistent and unpredictable family situations. It is a defense against our shame. Feeling a sense of control gives a sense of power at the time in our lives when we are overwhelmed by our powerlessness, helplessness, and fear. Giving up control as an adult is difficult when up to this point in life it has been of great value.

> Sit back in a comfortable seat and relax. Breathe deeply.
> Uncross your legs and arms. Gently close your eyes and reflect back in time to your growing-up years.
> Recognizing how you exerted control externally or internally, finish this sentence:
> *Giving up control in my family would have meant . . .*
> *Giving up control in my family would have meant . . .*
> *Giving up control in my family would have meant . . .*
> *Giving up control in my family would have meant . . .*
> *Giving up control in my family would have meant . . .*

If you have difficulty with this exercise, another way to benefit from it is to describe the controlling behavior. (Remember, controlling behavior was developed to protect you, so don't be judgmental.)

For example:

Not taking care of my mother would have meant . . .

—or—

Not doing the grocery shopping would have meant . . .

—or—

Not holding in my feelings would have meant . . .

Repeating these sentences allows you to access a deeper level of honesty. Now ask yourself if control means the same thing to you today.

As we become aware of the frightening connotation that the issue of control has for us, it is equally important to remind ourselves of the positive aspects that come with letting go of some control. It is in giving up *some* control that we genuinely become empowered.

In asking those in recovery to name what they experienced as they let go of control they responded:

- peace, serenity
- relaxation
- ability to listen to others
- ability to listen to ourselves
- trust in ourselves
- lack of fear
- spontaneity
- creativity
- fun, play
- energy
- our present feelings
- intimacy with self and others

These are the rewards, the promises of recovery.

As you reshape your life, you can retain pride in your ability to accomplish, but you also need to develop a greater sense of spontaneity and a greater ability to interact with others in a less rigid manner. You will be able to give up some areas of control only after you learn to identify your feelings and express these feelings in a manner that feels safe to you.

Adjuster

The adjusting child found it easier not to question, think about, nor respond in any way to what was occurring in his or her life. Adjusters do not attempt to change, prevent, or alleviate any situations. They simply "adjust" to what they are told, often by detaching themselves emotionally, physically, and socially as much as is possible.

While it is easier to survive the frequent confusion and hurt of a dysfunctional home through adjusting, there are many negative consequences for the adjusters in adult life.

Example: "As a result of adjusting/detaching, I got into a lot of strange situations because I didn't stop to think."

Complete the following:

As a result of adjusting/detaching, I ______________________________

____

because ____

____

____

As a result of adjusting/detaching, I ______________________________

____

because ____

____

____

As a result of adjusting/detaching, I ______________________________

____

because ____

____

____

As a result of adjusting/detaching, I ______________________________

____

because ____

____

____

The children who were more detached, possibly more nondescript than the responsible, placating, or acting-out children, are the adjusters. They need to take a look at how they feel about themselves. The adjusters have operated on the premise that "life is easier if you don't draw attention to yourself." They need to give themselves new messages which communicate that they are very important people and they deserve attention for themselves because they are very special. Adjusters have many feelings that they have not had the opportunity to examine and feelings that they have not had the opportunity to share with others.

Adjusting adults continue to survive usually by living their lives in a very malleable fashion. They need to recognize that at times it is healthier and more satisfying to be less flexible. Because adjusters make very few waves for other people, they have no sense of direction for themselves. They lack purpose or a feeling of fulfillment. It is like always just being along for the ride—one feels a sense of movement, yet often, one travels only in circles.

One adult child revealed that her husband decided to move five times, taking her to five states, in the first four years of their marriage. She said she didn't realize she could have discouraged any of the moves and, in fact, could have refused to go. She said she always did what he wanted. In retrospect, her adjusting was not good for her husband or for their relationship.

If you are such an adjusting adult, you need daily practice in identifying the power you have in your life. Here is a four-part exercise that will help you do just that.

Part 1. At the beginning of each day, write down at least five options you have that day.

For example:

1. I choose whether or not I eat breakfast.
2. I choose where I buy gas for the car.
3. I choose whom I sit with at lunch.
4. I choose which television show I watch.
5. I choose the time I go to bed.

Recognize that these five options are certainly not major decisions, but in the beginning, it is wise to start with the small areas of daily life one can change. This exercise should be done consistently for a period of one week.

Part 2. Continue this exercise for a second week, listing ten choices that can be made on a daily basis. The goal of this exercise is to teach you to acknowledge your power in making choices. By the third or fourth day, you will begin to feel the power.

Part 3. After following through with Part 2, practice on a daily basis making notes of existing options that were not acted upon. List three per day. Continue this part of the exercise for one week.
For example:

1. I did not speak up when I was shortchanged $1.60 at the grocery store.
2. I allowed my daughter to use the car for the evening when I wanted to use it.
3. I didn't tell my friends I disliked Japanese food when they suggested we eat at a sushi restaurant for my birthday.

The purpose of Part 3 is to recognize situations in which we did not act on our power.

Part 4. After each day's documentation, make a log of what could be done differently should the situation occur again. Even if you do not take that different action, list a few alternative responses. Should other alternatives not come to mind, another person—a friend, a therapist, someone that you respect—may be able to recommend an option.

Practice Parts 3 and 4 together for another week. They can be repeated as often as you feel the need.

Discuss this process with another, share the fun of having so many choices, and allow yourself to feel some pride in this new awareness.

If you are an adjuster who is attempting to change, watch for certain clues.

Should you begin to experience boredom, depression, or a sense of helplessness, it is time to become reacquainted with power and options. Practice the aforementioned exercise again.

Placater

The placater, otherwise known as the "household social worker" or "caretaker," was the child who was busy taking care of everyone else's emotional needs. This may be the young girl who perceives her sister's embarrassment when Mom shows up at a school open house drunk and will do whatever is necessary to take the embarrassment away. This may be a boy assisting his brother in not feeling the disappointment of Dad not showing up at a ball game. This is the child who intervenes and assures that his siblings are not too frightened after there has been a screaming scene. This is a warm, sensitive, listening, caring person who shows a tremendous capacity to help others feel better. For the placater, survival was taking away the fears, sadnesses, and guilt of others. Survival was giving one's time, energy, and empathy.

But as adults, people who have spent years taking care of others begin to "pay a price" for the "imbalance of focus." It is most likely that there were things that were not learned.

Example: "As a result of being the 'household social worker,' I didn't have time to tell anyone my problems because I was too busy assisting in solving other people's problems."

Complete the following:

As a result of being the "household social worker," I didn't have time to ____
because ____
____
____

As a result of being the "household social worker," I didn't have time to ____
because ____
____
____

As a result of being the "household social worker," I didn't have time to ______________________________
because ______________________________
____
____

As a result of being the "household social worker," I didn't have time to ______________________________
because ______________________________
____
____

For adult children who spend so much time taking care of other people's needs, it is important to understand the word "selfish." They have perfected the inability to give to themselves or consider their own needs. The placater's role is always to attend to the feelings and wants of another. As adult placaters proceed in recovery, it is natural for them to feel guilty for focusing on themselves.

"When I decide to put myself first for a change, I feel very guilty and have trouble differentiating between putting myself first and being selfish."

Remember, you are learning how to give to yourself, and that is not bad. In order to be willing to give to yourself, it is vital to look at old messages that may need to be changed.

New messages may be:

- I don't have to take care of everyone else.
- I have choices about how I respond to people.
- My needs are important.
- I have feelings; I'm scared; I am angry.
- It is okay to put my own well-being first.
- Some situations can be resolved without my being involved.
- Others can lend support to those who need it when I am not willing to be available.
- I'm not guilty because others feel bad.

This should only be the beginning of a list of new messages. To the adult placater, I suggest you find the messages that fit your situation and make a list of them. On a daily basis for a minimum of a month, read and reread these messages aloud to yourself.

You will feel some of the old guilt for a while, but it will be mixed with a new sensation—that of excitement along with a sense of aliveness. I believe in people giving themselves credit and being their own best friend, so do not be embarrassed about stroking yourself and being important to you.

Fifty-four-year-old Maureen said she spent her life trying to be everybody's "good little girl." She walked a very narrow line, afraid to do anything that might cause anyone's disapproval. "Slowly, I have learned it is much more important for me to consider my own needs and feelings, and how important it is for me to act on them." This is the type of freedom all adult children can attain. Maureen knows the process is slow. It is not easy to give up fears and try new behaviors. But, it is possible!

If you think you fit into the placater's role, examine how you give. On a daily basis, document all the little things you do for people. Itemize each one. After you have read your list of anywhere from fifty to a hundred items, are you tired? Of course you are tired. Where will you find the energy to give to yourself? The answer—you won't. Ask yourself if each of these placating acts was absolutely necessary. Could you have backed off a little? As you attempt to back off on giving, you need to start work on being able to receive. All true placaters need to work on receiving.

Ask yourself about your capacity to receive. Do you "yes, but . . ." when you are complimented? Do you change the subject when you are commended? Are you embarrassed or do you feel awkward when you receive a gift? Can you enjoy the moment? You may need to give yourself new messages regarding receiving:

- I deserve to be given a thank-you.
- I can enjoy being the recipient of praise.
- I will take time to hear my praise, smile, and soak it in.

For a minimum of two weeks, pay strict attention to receiving. Practice your new messages.

Acting-Out Child

Some kids in unhealthy homes became very angry at a young age. They were confused and scared and acted out their confusion in ways that got them a lot of negative attention. It was common that they got into trouble at home, school, and often on the streets. These are kids who were screaming, "There's something wrong here!" These are kids who didn't find survivorship in the other three roles.

Example: "As a result of my acting-out behavior, I didn't have time to pay attention at school."

Complete the following:

As a result of my acting-out behavior, I didn't have time to

____

____

____

As a result of my acting-out behavior, I didn't have time to

____

____

____

As a result of my acting-out behavior, I didn't have time to

____

____

____

As a result of my acting-out behavior, I didn't have time to

____

____

____

It is easy to scapegoat yourself for being in this role, yet creativity, flexibility, honesty, and humor are but a few of the strengths often shown by people who adopted this stance. Make a list of characteristics you value about yourself. If not taken to an extreme, they are most likely strengths.

Adult Roles

Today as an adult I am still (check the appropriate boxes):

- ☐ Overly responsible
- ☐ Placating
- ☐ Adjusting
- ☐ Acting out negatively
- ☐ Other ______________________________

As a result, I still haven't learned ______________________________
____
____
____

It is important for me to take the time to (be specific) ______________
____
____
____

This chapter is about taking risks. The reality is in reading this book you are taking risks. List five risks you have taken in the past that you feel good about. They could be risks at work, in your family, or as a part of a love relationship. Name the risk. What did you fear? What did you do, say, or think to get yourself to push through the fear and take the risk?

Many people attempting to make changes sometimes fear they will go to the other extreme. While the internal experience may feel extreme, the behavior is usually not.

As you change role patterns by being more spontaneous and more willing to follow (the responsible one), by making more decisions and being more assertive (adjuster), by giving more to yourself (placater), and by acknowledging your creativity (acting-out role), others will be responding to the new you in a variety of ways. Remember, they also have choices about how they respond. Many will welcome the change and adjust accordingly in the relationship. Those who want to manipulate you in order to have their needs met may attempt to sabotage your efforts. Recognize that they also have some fear about the change, about how you relate to them. However others respond, you will like yourself better as you develop the ability to give to yourself a part of your wholeness that has been denied for too long. Keep in mind that you deserve your gift to yourself.

Chapter 8

The Child within the Home

Children are not immune from the effects of addiction. They live with it and therefore need to understand it. Understanding addiction helps locate the problem and put it where it rightfully belongs. Understanding it also reduces their anxiety by making the unexpected predictable. It allows them to remove themselves from the line of fire. Knowing that the family is responding to a sickness allows the child to remain more guilt free because an illness is not something they can cause. When children realize a parent is addicted, it gives them the freedom to filter and evaluate the information a disturbed parent passes along. Most significantly, it gives a name to their experience and it says they aren't at fault. It gives them a voice with which to talk about their experiences.

These are often children who grow up never having shared their closest thoughts or feelings with even their very best friend. It is a very lonely, isolated way to live. This loneliness continues into adulthood because no one understood their trauma or was willing to take the time to talk to them. When we break the dysfunctional family rules, we begin offering children a framework for understanding what they are experiencing.

Children of all ages can comprehend addiction if the concepts are explained in a language they understand. Adults need to talk openly and provide children with access to literature that reinforces healthy messages. (See Suggested Reading in the appendix.)

This chapter covers the concepts that need to be discussed with children.

Addiction as a Disease

It is advisable to ask children what they think chemical dependency or addiction is and what traits constitute an alcoholic or addict. Children have undoubtedly heard the phrases from a friend, another family member, or through the media. These words are often used judgmentally and negatively.

It is vital they understand that the addicted family member is sick and suffering from a disease. Chemical dependency is not a disease caused by a germ or virus, as are many other diseases, but it is an illness nonetheless. People do not choose to become addicted and all the willpower in the world will not cure addiction. When they can understand that the chemically dependent person is one who cannot stop drinking or using without help because he or she is physically and psychologically addicted to a drug, you are beginning to help them view their parent and addiction in a more constructive light. They need to understand that addiction is evident in people who can no longer predict their behavior when drinking or using, who cannot control their use, and who have problems in their lives due to drinking or using.

Telling children they are more prone to become alcoholic or addicted to other substances or behaviors won't prevent them from developing addiction. While this information is valuable to them, it is unrealistic to expect them to choose not to drink or use because of knowledge alone. Unfortunately, this information will not necessarily be sufficient for them to identify drinking or using as a problem prior to becoming chemically dependent. Children raised with addiction require more than just information. They need psychological, emotional, physical, and social intervention, understanding, and support.

Blackouts

Blackouts are periods of amnesia, varying in duration from minutes to several hours or, for some people, several days. The alcoholic, who is conscious and drinking at the time, will have no recall later about the events which occurred during that portion of time.

Imagine a Friday night when Dad doesn't come home for dinner and still isn't home when everyone has gone to bed. When he finally does arrive, he makes a lot of noise and argues with his thirteen-year-old daughter, whom he meets in the hallway as she heads for the bathroom. Dad then proceeds to awaken Mom and the two of them argue loudly for several hours in their bedroom. The next day Dad remembers only drinking with his friends and anticipating that his wife would be angry because he was late for dinner. His recollection stops somewhere in the early evening. He doesn't remember exactly when he got home or talking with anyone in the family. The two younger children show some anxiety around Dad and are apprehensive of his mood the next morning. The thirteen-year-old acts abrupt with him. Dad doesn't know why she behaves this way and is fearful of asking. Rather than risk finding out, he treats her with a placating attitude. Mom acts like everything is okay. No one talks about the real issues—Dad's behavior the night before, the confusion, the fear, and the disappointment. In a family already fragmented, more distance and misunderstanding are created.

When children understand blackouts and that Dad really may have no recall, they will have the option of checking Dad's memory and pointing out to him what occurred during his blackout. There will be less confusion and fear when the child realizes Dad won't be as likely to proceed with the same argument if he has no recall of that argument. Understanding blackouts makes it easier for children to cope with the parent's illness.

Some children may suspect that their parent, when drinking, actually does not remember a period of time, such as a segment of what happened the night before. Other children who have no knowledge of blackouts experience an even greater sense of confusion and craziness about what happens in the home. Whether or not children recognize when blackouts occur, they need to have some information and an explanation that validates their own experience and allows them to have a better understanding of their parent's denial. This validation also provides an avenue, or permission, to talk about it.

Personality Changes

The Jekyll-and-Hyde phenomenon is certainly witnessed by family members and is not due to craziness, but is, in fact, caused by drinking or using. Many people believe when major personality changes occur, they are the result of mental illness. This happens because many addicts have been labeled and diagnosed as schizophrenic and psychotic. Personality changes and drastic mood swings for addicts are due to their alcohol and drug use. Children need to be made aware that alcohol and drugs can cause a total change in personality, and that not all people who exhibit such behavior are mentally ill.

The nonaddicted parent also demonstrates personality changes. Preoccupation with the addict and the fluctuation of feelings associated with the preoccupation may create very irrational responses. The nonaddicted parent needs to let the children know he or she is doing his or her best to be more predictable. So, hopefully, the only unpredictability will be that of the addict's behavior. Acknowledging that problems in the home are a reality, coupled with renewed attempts to provide consistency, will create much more stability for the children.

MY DADDY GOES AWAY
SOMETIMES

SARAH 14

Broken Promises

Broken promises are a common reality for children of an addicted parent. They are often told they will be going someplace, or a parent will attend a school event, or they will be given something, only to have the addict not follow through. This usually occurs with no accountability or apology. It is important that children know their feelings, such as anger and disappointment, are valid. Children need to be taught promises are broken because of the parent's addiction, not because of a lack of caring or loving. The preoccupation with drinking or using becomes the addict's number one priority. All else is secondary.

Denial

Denial can be explained as the time someone minimizes, diminishes, rationalizes, or simply denies certain behavior, thoughts, or feelings. Denial occurs when people pretend things are different than they really are. The addicted person often denies in order to protect their addiction. The addict denies how much they drank or used, where they were, or whom they hurt.

Family members also deny. The spouse and children deny in an attempt to believe in their "addict" to make things easier for them or other family

members. They minimize and rationalize their feelings and thoughts, saying things like "It didn't hurt," when it did; "I wasn't angry," when they were; "He didn't know what he was doing," when he did.

Enabling

Children need to learn that it is not okay to make excuses or to lie in an attempt to cover up for the addict's behavior. Spouses and children often lie to . . . clean up after . . . make excuses for . . . bail out . . . the addicted person.

Family members enable because they feel they must, or because they don't want to risk the unpleasant results of the addict becoming upset, or because it simply makes home life easier. There are endless numbers of reasons for enabling behavior. The result of enabling is that the addict does not see and does not address the consequences of drinking or using behavior. Enabling behavior actually makes it easier for the chemically dependent person to continue their addictive behavior.

Relapse

A nine-year-old whose mother was alcoholic most eloquently stated a definition of relapse.

> *"A relapse is when you stop drinking and then you start again. It's like when you have a cold and you think it is gone. Then you go out in the rain and your cold comes back."*
>
> —Melody

Relapses are not unusual in that they can, and do, occur in most progressive diseases. In a disease such as cancer, there are times when the cancer appears to be arrested; it is not progressing. Then, it begins its process again, and the cancer patient is said to have had a relapse. When someone has pneumonia and recovers, often they suffer a relapse and become sick again.

Relapse is a term that needs to be discussed if a parent attempts to get clean and sober. Many parents ask, "Why worry the child?" The reality is the child is already worried. The child's worries are validated and less overwhelming if this concern is discussed.

However, family members need to go about their daily activities without being preoccupied with the possibility of relapse. In discussing relapse, it is necessary for children to understand they don't cause relapses. Even if it appears that the sixteen-year-old son's wrecking the family car precipitated Dad's relapse, Dad must learn to cope with such problems, or uncomfortable feelings, without reaching for his drug. The addict is not guilty for having the disease but is responsible for the decision to drink or use again. There is much he or she needs to learn to do in order to prevent relapse, and other family members can best understand this through their own involvement in a recovery program.

These basic concepts can also be applied to other addictive disorders. Addictions, whether to substances or behaviors, have identifiable symptoms and stages, and the addict experiences a denial system and demonstrates personality changes. The family learns ways to enable the behavior. Relapse is common in their recovery process. The child is not at fault, nor responsible for the recovery.

MY DADDY
I woke up one morning and he was gone
he was gone my daddy
and he would never be home again.
He was gone my daddy
the one who always showed his love the one who always understood,
when she never would!
The one who always brushed my hair,
combed and put ribbons in my hair
he was the one who picked me up
when I fell and skinned my knee.
Oh my daddy, my daddy.
I still remember all the things he taught me—but he was gone.
And I was too young to understand
he said they just didn't get along.
I hardly ever saw him,
my daddy who was always there,
my daddy who always cared.

It seemed he just didn't have time for me. But that was also ten years ago and I think
now I understand.
But there's still one question that remains. And that's—
Why Oh Lord, did this have to happen to me???
Why did my daddy have to go, and leave me all alone?
She says he's alcoholic, a person who has a disease and needs help . . .
But can only get it if he wants it.
He must admit to himself that he is sick and needs help.
he knows all this now and I do too.
Now it's too late, he's already gone.
He's remarried now and he has a new little princess
who he brushes, combs, and puts ribbons in her hair.
But Lord this is so unfair!!!
He is my daddy and he needs help!!!
But I feel so helpless Lord because
it seems he still doesn't have time for me.
I love my daddy, whom I hardly ever see.
And even more when I think about
how much he must Love Me—MY DADDY

—Renee, age 16

Children raised with addiction experience loss as a result of the parents not being consistently available to them. This is a natural loss as a result of the chemically dependent person's preoccupation with their need to drink or use and the coaddict's preoccupation with the addict. When children experience loss, they enter a grief process, one similar to the grief processes other people experience when they lose a loved one due to death, or when a loved one becomes incapacitated because of a serious illness.

The first state of grief is disbelief, or denying the loss has really occurred. The disbelief may be nature's way of helping a person through this stage by deadening the pain, by giving a person time to absorb the facts. Unfortunately, with chemical dependency, this grief process is much slower, occurring over a much longer time and in a much more subtle way. As a result, family members are often in a state of disbelief for a lengthy time.

With addiction, as time passes and the truth becomes more evident, the family begins to experience the terror . . . the terror of the reality that a loved one is an addict. Usually, the next emotion following the terror is anger. "If you (the addict) really love me, how can you be like this?" The family members often feel guilt. Each family member believes that in some way they are responsible. A son believes: "Maybe if I hadn't talked back, Dad wouldn't drink so much or be so angry all the time." A wife believes: "If I were a better wife, my husband wouldn't be sick." A husband believes: "Maybe if I had been home more . . ." Bargaining is practiced by family members when they elicit promises from the drinker to control or stop the drinking. At other times, bargaining is self-imposed: "If I behave this way, maybe Mom will respond another way." For many children the bargaining is through prayer: "Please God, keep my mom and dad together. Don't let them fight so much. I promise I will be real good." Finally, family members feel desperation and despair.

They each feel alone with the problem. They feel all these terrible things are unique in their lives, that no one else could possibly understand their pain. They despair that there are no answers or solutions to the guilt they carry. This process and these feelings are common to all persons affected by the addictions.

Families that try to run away from their feelings suffer longer. Often, they never recover from their grief, and it becomes a long lasting depression. Families who face loss, and the related feelings, become stronger and will be able to begin growing, living full and satisfying lives.

A child can survive a family crisis as long as he or she is told the truth and allowed to share the natural sequence of feelings people experience when they suffer. In addictive families, everyone suffers, and everyone suffers very much alone. Children often suffer from loneliness, fear, anger, and a multitude of other feelings that they have no way of understanding. Furthermore, they do not have the ability to express this lack of understanding.

Although the child may receive help to understand addiction, intellectual understanding will not erase the multitude of intense feelings they experience. Children can understand and feel at the same time. It is important for someone to explain that his or her feelings are perfectly normal. Children need to be able to say, "I was so embarrassed. I know she is sick, but she still embarrasses me and it hurts!" Or, "I'm sad because Mom is like she is. But, I'm also really angry, and I don't understand why she won't go for help!" All of these feelings are valid. They need to know others will validate and listen to their feelings. The nonaddicted parent, along with outside resources, can fill this necessary validating role.

Crying

Crying is a natural release of emotions. Children and spouses both need to cry. Crying is difficult for many people, but those in addicted families usually do one of two things: they learn how not to cry or cry alone, very silently.

Before a child can cry and feel okay about it, the child needs to be given healthy messages regarding crying: "It's okay to cry" and "Crying will help you to feel better." Other messages, such as "Boys shouldn't cry" and "Don't be a crybaby," need to be countered. Children also need models who can demonstrate that crying is not weak or shameful. If a parent is in recovery, he or she needs to model the healthy expression of feelings and to talk openly about this new change in behavior. Children need to hear that when adults hurt they too cry. And that when family members show each other their tears, it is often a time in which they can feel closer to each other. Aside from giving permission to cry, children need support to share their feelings with others. Ask children whom they could tell about the times when they cry? Whom do they trust enough to confide in? Whom in the family do they trust to ask for comfort at such times? This can be a very valuable discussion.

I once worked with a brother and sister, six-year-old Chuck and nine-year-old Melody. Chuck was very open about not trusting his mother and his helplessness regarding her drinking. He talked about worrying a lot, and at times, he cried when he talked. Melody would tell him to shut up. She would talk louder when he was speaking and would call him a crybaby. She was prepared to do just about anything she could to keep Chuck from talking and showing his feelings. Though there was only three years difference in their ages, Chuck and Melody were in different stages of denial. It is important for adults to be aware of these varying stages of denial among children and how children interfere with or are supportive of each other's expressions of feelings. One child may be more open to expression of tears, while another is obviously angry; still another child appears simply to be nonfeeling. Each child needs to have access to all of their feelings and have healthy avenues of expression.

Fear

While fear is a natural emotion for all children, it is, unfortunately, pervasive in an addictive family. A parent's drinking or using results in a lot of tension in the home and it's important a child's fears are acknowledged and validated. Whether or not children express specific fears, parents, family, and friends need to validate that at times it is quite reasonable to be afraid. Many times, nothing can be done about what is creating the fear, yet acknowledging it can lessen the power. Expressing feelings develops closeness between parents and children and is helpful in decreasing the children's feelings of being overwhelmed by the emotions kept inside. Emotions become so much more powerful when they are not outwardly expressed. Keeping feelings hidden can cause a great deal more pain than is necessary.

Anger

Anger is a normal feeling. Everyone experiences it. Yet due to punishment, the possibility of rejection, or fear of abuse, many children are reticent to own or share their anger. It is extremely important for children to become aware of their frustrations and angers and then find ways to express them. Children's anger is only problematic when it has been stored and appropriate ways of expression have not been introduced.

Ask children what happens when family members get angry. In doing this, you are asking them how they perceive the way anger is expressed at home. Their responses will guide you in determining what needs to be addressed. When nine-year-old Mike was asked what people in his family do with anger, he said, "Dad leaves the house. Mom drinks. Tommy goes outside. I'm not really angry." Mike was a very overweight young boy, and his description demonstrated how he had copied his mother's pattern for coping with anger, while his brother copied his father's pattern. Two family members leave their anger behind, and two drink or eat to cope with it. None of them found a healthy way of coping with anger.

To feel safe in expressing anger, children need to know their anger will not cause them to lose their parent's love. For so many people, expressing anger has come to mean "If I show you I'm angry with you, you will withdraw your love." Children need to know what limits are placed on the expression of anger and what others perceive as appropriate responses to situations.

Children need to know their hurts and angers are very important and should not be discounted. Children often discount problems in their own lives because they believe problems taking place within the family structure take precedence over any personal conflicts occurring outside the home. "Who am I to talk about how angry I became at school today? There is already enough tension at home."

The messages learned are:

1. What happened to me at school is not important.
2. The feelings I have throughout the day at school are not important.
3. I am not important.

Children need to have their feelings validated, whether big or small.

Guilt

Children assume they have the power to affect everything, when in truth, they have very little power in an addictive environment. "Dad was always screaming and hollering about us kids never doing anything right, so I assumed we had to be making him very unhappy and that was why he took off and didn't come home." Children need to know they do not cause someone to be addicted. Children need to be reassured that even if they behave in a way that upsets a parent their parent has many choices other than drinking or using to handle the situation. Remind them no one but the addict is responsible for the alcoholic/addict's actions.

It is important for a child to be able to distinguish the difference between true and false guilt. True guilt is a feeling of regret or remorse for your own behavior. For example, a person is responsible for being late, lying, stealing, not following through on a commitment. False guilt is a feeling of remorse that come from believing you are responsible for someone else's behavior and actions.

Jim is forty-three years old. He described a Friday night when he was twelve. He said there was nothing unusual about this night. Mom had cooked dinner, he and Mom ate, and she put Dad's meal in the oven, even though both of them knew he wouldn't eat it when he arrived home. When Dad came home close to ten o'clock that night, he was intoxicated. He began his typical ranting and raving, as if he knew something about their day that they did not know. As he would usually do, Jim took the car keys and went to hide them so his dad couldn't go out again. This time was different, though. Jim broke his typical response. He walked back toward his father and threw the keys at him and hollered, "I wish you would just go kill yourself." Then Jim went to his room. Dad was startled, but in his anger, he grabbed his coat, yelled at his wife, and stomped out the door. Ten miles down the road Dad was in a one-car accident and died. Jim now believes he caused that accident and his father's death. This is a false guilt that he took with him well into adulthood. That night Jim was rightfully angry. He wished his father would die. But he did not cause his father to die. When you feel such futility, as did Jim, it is a normal response to wish that the person who creates so much pain would die. Instead of being able to be angry with his father and be sad for the relationship he will never have and for all the pain that has occurred, Jim takes on guilt that is not his.

Children feel guilt not only because they think they are the cause of problems, or because they cannot remedy the problem, but also because they have conflicting feelings about anger and love. Children learn early in childhood that they are expected to love and respect their parents. When someone's number one priority is to drink or use, he or she is incapable of acting in ways that demonstrate or accept love. Love consists of mutual respect, trust, and sharing, all the characteristics an addict loses for himself and for others. A parent's inability to love and accept love is both frustrating and confusing for children. It is very understandable for children to be confused about loving a parent who is frightening, unavailable, or inconsistent.

Children have to be helped to understand that feelings are transitory. One may feel intense hatred for a person, then, at another time, feel empathy. One may experience great tenderness toward a person and become enraged at them a few hours later. Feelings change, and children will not be "stuck" with a feeling forever. Most children do not realize this by themselves; it must be explained to them in terms they can understand.

Children need to know it is possible to experience more than one feeling at a time. Sadness and anger can be felt together, as can happiness and sadness, fear and anxiety, love and hate. There are numerous combinations. What's important is that the adult be accepting of the child's feelings, even if the child says, "I don't love Mom. I hate her." If adults can accept and validate children's feelings of intense dislike, as well as anger, fear, and disappointment, then they can also help children to live lives free of guilt for having these feelings. We can help children work through these feelings and, hopefully, acquire a more positive acceptance of themselves.

It is important to acknowledge that children do love their parents. Love frequently withstands a lot of inconsistent, painful parenting. The love that is felt often relates to the experiences shared prior to the onset of addiction, as well as to the sober moments shared. Addicted parents are not under the influence all the time. Addiction is a process, the onset of which most often begins in a person's mid-twenties or early thirties. This indicates that most parents begin raising their children in preaddicted or early addictive years.

When a person is in the early stages, the behavior may not be consistently disruptive to the family. The same is true for the nonaddicted parent. It is over time that nonaddicted parents become depressed, angry, rigid, or absent. The codependent behavior was not necessarily typical of them in the early stages. They too were often more consistent and provided more quality time for the children. The love children feel was often internalized in those earlier years.

It is my bias that while we cannot make children love their parents, we can help them not to hate. It is easier for children not to "get stuck" in hate if we can provide more consistency in their lives, as well as educating them to better understand addiction and its effects on the entire family structure.

Children usually learn about feelings and what to do with them by modeling adults. The more healthy role models that are available, the greater the ability children have to adopt that healthy behavior and utilize positive avenues of expression. The more isolated the family becomes, the fewer options children have to learn from healthy adults. Children need access to healthy role models.

We will not be able to attend to each and every feeling that a child experiences. But, if we consistently offer healthy messages and validations and model ways to cope with feelings, children won't need constant support for every feeling they experience.

Manipulativeness

Children quickly learn they have power over certain situations in their lives and use this knowledge to their own advantage. Some children recognize they have the power to manipulate the addict during times of personality changes, remorse, and blackouts. "I know Dad will let me out Saturday night, no questions asked, after he's been drinking. So, I'll wait until late Friday night to ask. If I ask earlier, he'll be more sober and he'll ask me twenty questions about what I am doing." Or, ask Mom for your allowance when she is drinking and she will give you twenty dollars instead of five. The same tactics will also be used with the codependent parent. Children prey on the guilt of the codependent parent as much as they prey on the obliviousness of the addicted parent. Children are children, and their manipulativeness can be expected as a normal part of their growing-up process. But with healthy boundaries on the part of the nonaddicted parent, this can be lessened. It is important to intervene when you see the manipulativeness and be direct with the kids about not preying on the sickness of the addict.

Problem Solving

An important positive result of talking about feelings is that it can lead to healthier problem solving. Suppose this coming Friday, Sally has an important mother-daughter function, and Mom's attendance is dependent on whether or not she drinks or uses that day. Though Sally has not approached her father with her fears, he can approach Sally saying, "I know your function is on Friday, and I'm sure it is important to you. Your mother told me about it herself last night. You're probably concerned as to whether or not she'll really attend." At that point, the parent should stop and listen. Give Sally a chance to respond. Be it a parent, concerned friend, or counselor, it is very appropriate to problem solve with her. Ask, "Have you thought about what you'll do if your mother is drinking or using then?" Then listen. Offer possibilities should she need such guidance. Certainly, the possibilities include: 1) Sally would not go; 2) she would go alone; 3) she would ask another adult to attend in lieu of her mother; or 4) she would go with a friend and her friend's mother. It is important that Sally not isolate herself as a result of her mother's addiction and that she continue with her plans as close to the original idea as possible. It is healthy to encourage the child to attend the function and to use an alternative support system. Problem solving is more likely to occur when feelings are discussed, both before and after an event.

Carrie, age six, came to her fifth children's group with her older brother, Tony, age eight, and proposed this problem: Their dad had returned to drinking since he left a treatment program five weeks earlier. They did not live with their dad and saw him only on weekends. They explained that even though Dad was drinking, he wasn't getting drunk, nor was he causing any problems. During this particular meeting, Carrie told us her dad promised to take her to Disneyland next weekend. She had been to Disneyland the year before and really liked it. Tony wouldn't be going along because he was taking a weekend trip with their mother. While Carrie wanted to go to Disneyland, she was scared her father would drink, ruining the trip.

Carrie loved her dad and wanted to be with him and she wanted to go to Disneyland—but she was also frightened. She was scared of being embarrassed should her father drink, and she feared his ability to drive safely on the ninety-minute trip home. On the other hand, she felt a need to protect her father and didn't want to hurt his feelings by telling him he frightens her. Carrie further believes that if she told her father why she is afraid, he would stop taking her places and would not want to see her at all. She clearly felt she was in a no-win situation.

Carrie didn't want to share her fears with her mother, because her mother might not let her go to Disneyland at all, and Carrie knew she couldn't go on the weekend trip with Mom and Tony. Finally, she said, "It's all so complicated. I will just go and maybe he won't drink anyway." Carrie was both concerned and exasperated about her dilemma.

In the same group, Trisha, age eleven, who also goes to her dad's house on weekends told us, "Dad goes out in the evenings and drinks; he stays out real late!" Trisha said she stays alone during these evenings, worrying about her dad and crying a lot. Trisha feels she can't make her dad stay home, yet she doesn't want to tell her mother, who may not let her spend weekends at her father's.

While these are certainly not the most severe problems encountered by young children, they are representative of the dilemmas children usually face in trying to resolve problems by themselves.

For Trisha and Carrie, there are not any clear-cut satisfactory answers for such problems. But, all children need an adult, preferably a parent, to 1) offer them guidance, 2) protect them, and 3) give them permission to protect themselves.

Children can be offered these basic messages: 1) the addicted parent who is still using will not always be able to make the best decisions, and 2) it is important and permissible to ask others for help.

Children can better handle problems and protect themselves if necessary when they have the time to discuss and think over potential situations. When children have been briefed on possible situations, given positive messages about themselves, and believe an adult will support them, they will usually choose better options.

In Trisha's and Carrie's case, each girl eventually decided she wanted to go with her father. We adults need to understand the children's need and love for their parent.

Situations	Possibilities
Carrie's "WHAT IF . . ." Carrie's problem—fear that Dad will go to Disneyland and drink. Fear of embarrassment, and Dad's drunken driving. But she decides to go.	Tell Dad about concerns prior to going, and ask him to try not to drink. Ask Dad to take a specific adult friend (one you know and suggest) for protection.
Trisha decides for herself she wants to go to Dad's each weekend, but doesn't want to go alone, and feel bad. She's asked him to stay home on evenings, but that hasn't worked.	Tell Dad I love him and want him to stay with me since I only see him on weekends. Take games with me knowing I will probably be alone at night. Tell Dad I want to have a friend spend nights with me if he is going to go out.

The following examples are strategies that were discussed with children who needed to protect themselves from dangerous or vulnerable situations.

Situations	Possibilities
Child's "WHAT IF . . ." I am with Dad, 40 minutes from home, and his driving is scaring me. He doesn't seem drunk, but he has had at least six beers in the last two hours.	Tell him his driving scares me and ask him to slow down, or pull over. (This request is only likely to work if Dad has been forewarned of it. It may not be an option if Dad is more likely to become angry.) If he pulls the car over, or if I ask him to pull the car over, I will call the other parent or friend (a person already designated and who has agreed to help when available). Someone will come and pick me up.

The role of the concerned adult during the problem-solving session is twofold:

1. To provide guidance and offer suggestions so children realize they *do* have alternative choices.
2. To reassure children that they will have support in these choices, and that their choices will not be discounted, nor will they be punished for their feelings.

While these possibilities are not always workable, children need to know they are not expected to stay in a situation that frightens them, and if they choose alternatives, other caring adults will support their actions.

It is important to remember these are merely options, not necessarily suggestions or recommendations. Each family unit knows its situation best. What is important here is the process of identifying potential and actual problems, and then seeking viable options.

Obviously, children are more likely to use an option if they know they will be supported and a positive response from another adult will follow. This discussion approach is a major step that will begin breaking down the addict's denial process and will eliminate the rules of Not Talking, Not Feeling, and Not Trusting.

Adult family members also have "What If's."

Situations	Possibilities
Parent's "WHAT IF . . ." I fear the addict will start a fire as she smokes while severely intoxicated. She has burned holes in the furniture.	Get fire alarm for house. Identify escape routes. Have fire drill. Provide another adult to stay with the children or have children stay at another home. (Do not allow children to sit in fear.)
Adult child "WHAT IF . . ." I don't want to go to parents' for Christmas due to Mom's usual drunkenness at this time. I don't want Dad to be alone, yet don't want children to experience another Christmas with drunken grandmother.	Invite Dad to come alone for the Christmas gathering, and tell him why. Go for limited time, two hours versus all day. Extend an invitation to Mom to come to your house. She knows your rule, "No drinking."

If the addict is not present when the problem-solving possibilities are discussed, it can be helpful to tell him or her about the family's plan of action. Be sure the addict knows his or her behavior (as a result of addiction) is perceived as a problem and/or possibly a major threat to the family's safety. The Problem Solving Form in the appendix may be very helpful in conducting a problem-solving discussion.

Encourage Connections

Children grow up to be just like their parents or to have a variation of their parents' dysfunction unless someone shows them a different way. It is important for children to have a connection to others who validate the child for who he or she is, who help children to problem solve so they aren't problem solving in a vacuum. They need someone who engages them in activities that increase their self-esteem as well. Being involved in extra-curricular activities at school or church has proved to be of significant value in developing resiliency and strengths in response to a problematic life. Many adult children will talk about the role of an extended family member, a friend's parent, a school employee, or another person who made a difference in their life. Giving children access to resources that allow them not to be preoccupied with what is occurring at home, to see how other adults problem solve, and to tap into their individual talents is crucial for a child living in a troubled family.

Upon reflection, adult children in recovery can identify the people and their connection to them that fueled a part of their resiliency. Tom is convinced his involvement in high school sports was his time out from home and also a source of esteem. Ellie still sees her junior high school boyfriend's parents. She considers them as having been surrogate parents who listened, validated her, and allowed her to just be a kid. Lou believes it was his uncle, whom he describes as a quiet man, who took time to allow Lou in his life. He allowed Lou to help with chores around the house, go on short vacations with his family, and showed up at Lou's school events. The message Lou got was that he was of value to this uncle, that he was worthy. What can seem so little to the giver can make a tremendous difference to the receiver.

Create and Maintain Positive Family Rituals

Family rituals quickly become dismantled or hurtful for children in addictive families. Dinnertime is a time to be feared, bedtime is lonely. Rituals around Halloween are ignored. Christmas holidays are times of family scenes or being forgotten or dismissed. Birthday celebrations are times of great unpredictability. Celebrations such as high school graduation or bar mitzvahs are times of great trepidation because of the unpredictability or the unknown. There are possibilities for creating healthy rituals around mealtimes and bedtime, as well as specific celebrations or holidays. Whatever can be done to support this is most important.

Reshaping Roles

As described in chapter 4, "Progression of the Roles," the roles children adopt, whether it be responsible, adjusting, placating, or acting-out, lead them to have "gaps." Gaps are psychological voids that result from inconsistent parenting and lack of appropriate boundaries and emotional support. These voids are integrated into the children's social development and create major problems in adulthood. The gaps include not learning to relax, not knowing how to rely on others, not knowing how to follow, not knowing how to lead, never allowing one's own needs to be met, and many other undeveloped coping mechanisms. Not only will these gaps create life-skill problems, but they may also predispose the children to marry addicts and/or engage in addictive disorders. The lack of healthy coping mechanisms most often predisposes children to experience emotional problems.

When giving children an understanding of addiction through talking about the real issues and teaching them to identify and express feelings while establishing healthy support networks, there is also a specific need to focus on reshaping roles.

There are obvious benefits in learning how to be responsible, adjust, and placate, yet in this process, gaps are created because children have not acquired a sense of emotional balance. They adopt roles out of a severe need, a sense of survival, so they may bring consistency to an extremely chaotic and unpredictable family system. While we should not seek to take away the positive aspects of any role, we do need to help children achieve a better sense of balance in certain areas. In essence, we need to fill the gaps. Children need an environment in which they can learn social skills their natural survival techniques are not allowing them to learn.

The reshaping of roles generally means changing our expectations of children's behaviors and also changing our behavior toward them. Instead of becoming immediately frustrated when the eight-year-old acts eight years of age and insisting she act like a little adult, allow her to display some of that normal eight-year-old behavior. This will require patience. When the placating child reaches out to placate one more time, rather than applaud him, let him know you appreciate his thoughtfulness but you want to be alone and you are going to call an adult friend to talk.

Remember, change in any system, even when that change is positive, is often met with resistance. As you assist in reshaping roles, children may exhibit confusion, depression, withdrawal, or anger. Children will feel awkward about making changes, but these feelings are natural and are to be expected.

You can expect a certain amount of rebellion from a ten-year-old who has been busy playing "Mom" and "little adult" when you suggest she try to play hopscotch and giggle with her friends—behavior which has been totally out of her realm of reality.

A similar rebellion will come from the adjusting child when you ask him to share his anger or hurt. For this son, who managed to stare at the television while Dad was drunkenly ranting and raving and showed no signs of being affected, to share feelings now seems far beyond his present capabilities.

For the placating child, who has been taking care of everyone else's feelings, to become more selfish about her own feelings is a difficult task. Being self-focused does not give her the satisfaction she felt in taking care of others. She has not learned to feel good about herself when she is away from her charges. This becomes a very frightening time of adjustment for her.

Reshaping roles will be difficult whether or not the drinking or using has stopped. Role reshaping must be done slowly and it is more effective when several adults are involved in the process. Tell grandparents, extended family, neighbors, and school personnel how they can be helpful to the children.

In reshaping roles, the goal is not to take a responsible child and make him irresponsible, or an adjusting child and make her inflexible, or a placating child and make him totally egocentric, it is for the child to learn a balance of roles. We want them to experience choice when they respond to different situations.

It is important for all children to develop a sense of choice about where this responsibility lies. We need to help all children accept certain responsibilities for themselves and to reward them verbally for their accomplishments. While some children will take on more responsibility than others, it is very important not to allow one child to take on the surrogate or strong parenting role for the other children. For that overly responsible child, this may mean relieving him of the necessity to do certain "responsible" things and at the same time being supportive of other "fun" activities appropriate for a child his age. You may find yourself saying to Tom, "Mrs. Brown from next door will be here when your sister comes home from school today, so if you want, you can stay after school for about forty-five minutes and play." The changing of roles may mean spreading the areas of responsibility and it may mean providing others to share the responsible role the child previously held alone.

Spreading the responsibility may mean providing a baby-sitter, even though the ten-year-old is extremely responsible and nearly as capable as the fifteen-year-old baby-sitter. It could mean that the parent gets up twenty minutes earlier in the morning and prepares a casserole. This makes the adult responsible for dinner and not the twelve-year-old. Children need your support and encouragement to make friends and to be involved in after-school play activities. Applaud and encourage them to take time out to play and laugh.

Be careful not to deemphasize the importance of responsibility with overly responsible children. Instead, emphasize parts of their characters they have not yet actualized—their spontaneity, playfulness, and ability to lean on someone and to recognize that they are not compelled to have all the answers. It is okay to make mistakes. Responsible children need to be praised and have their deeds acknowledged not only when they are doing their best and acting as strong leaders, but also when other endeavors take them out of the leadership role, such as playing on a team without being the captain.

Remember, while these children demonstrate leadership qualities, this personality characteristic will be healthy only when it is not adopted as a matter of survival. Reinforce the children's natural need to share with and lean on others when they have to make decisions and work on projects. Let them know although they are bright and accomplished youngsters, they are still just that—youngsters. People of all ages need help, advice, and guidance at some points in their lives; these messages are best transmitted when both words and actions coincide.

Recommended reinforcing behaviors for responsible children:

- Give attention at times when the child is not achieving
- Validate the child's intrinsic worth, and try to separate their feelings of self-worth from their achievements
- Let the child know it's okay to make a mistake
- Encourage the child to play

With children who are not overly responsible, encourage them to take risks and make decisions for themselves. They need to learn to trust their own decision-making processes. They need to find when they do make a decision that you will follow through and support them. Start with situations that are the least threatening and have the fewest possible negative consequences—what television show to watch, what to have for dinner, how to handle a project. These children must learn to feel good about themselves because of their own accomplishments and their own decisions, not because they seek approval. Remember, the placating child will gladly make a decision if that is what is necessary to obtain approval. The goal, however, is not to attain approval, it is to instill in children the ability to make their own healthy decisions, to learn organizational skills, and to know how to problem solve.

As adjusting and placating children are taught a sense of leadership, the responsible children need to learn adjusting qualities. They will most likely learn to adjust only when they find others are capable and willing to provide direction for them. Until others demonstrate the willingness, responsible children won't trust relinquishing control.

As you help children identify and share feelings, you will need to spend more time with the placating child, reinforcing the fact that he or she is not responsible for another's feelings. For instance, when you were crying because your husband was verbally abusive, let your child know it hurt your feelings, and yes, you are sad, but the child is not responsible for your sadness. Share with your child that you are okay, but you've just had your feelings hurt.

Placating children need to learn to play, as do other children who take on adult roles. These children need a lot of reinforcement in order to learn it is okay to have their own needs met. Placating children become more stable when they know others are aware of and sensitive to the feelings in the home.

Recommended reinforcing behaviors for adjusting children:

- Engage in one-to-one contact to learn more about the individual child
- Point out and encourage the child's strengths, talents, and creativity
- Bring them into decision-making process, giving them win-win choices

Recommended reinforcing behaviors for placating children:

- Assist the child in focusing on themselves (instead of others)
- Help this child play
- When they are assisting another, ask them to identify how they are feeling and how they are feeling about the other person's situation
- Validate the child's intrinsic worth, separating their worth from their caretaking

For the acting-out child, recognize that this child is displaying unacceptable behavior because of 1) family problems, 2) the inability to have needs met, and 3) a lack of knowledge as to how to let others know what is wanted. Acting-out children were many times initially responsible and sensitive to others but found it brought them no satisfaction. The consequence of their dissatisfaction is rebellion—rebellion used to ward off pain. Many acting-out children have the ability to lead and can respond sensitively to others when in the right environment. These children must learn new productive outlets for anger; these children need validation and consistency in their lives.

Recommended reinforcing behaviors for acting-out children:

- Let the child know when behavior is inappropriate
- Give the child strokes whenever he or she takes responsibility for something
- Develop empathy for the child
- Set limits and give clear explanations of the child's responsibilities and clear choices and consequences

The Abstinent Home

Even though the addict may now be clean and sober or is no longer living with the family due to separation, divorce, or death, patterns don't stop because the blatant acting-out behavior has stopped or is no longer visible. Children, by themselves, do not recognize the need for change. People naively believe that if the addictive behavior stops or if the addict leaves the family then everything will be okay. Unfortunately, that is not the case.

I'm reminded of a nineteen-year-old who told me she continues to lie about insignificant events. She developed this pattern in an effort to bring stability to a very violent alcoholic home. When she told me this, the violent alcoholic parent had been out of the home for three years (due to divorce). She said she was not aware of her pattern of lying until recently, when she was confronted with the behavior. One reason family members do not change their ways after the addict has become sober or has left is because they seldom realize they have been adversely affected.

A forty-three-year-old recovering alcoholic told me that even after six years of sobriety he had not once talked to his children about his alcoholism or the effects it had on the family. He explained he now feels close to his children (two adult children in their early twenties and a fourteen-year-old) yet regrets that many things have been left unsaid. He recognizes the negative impact his addiction had on the family, but he doesn't know how to approach his children about the problems carried over from the past.

It definitely is awkward, after any number of years, to bring up these sensitive issues. However, in the long run, if the painful feelings and problems are not addressed, they become increasingly difficult to resolve. This closeting of feelings creates a distance and perpetuates a lack of communication among family members. The ability to deny is likely to continue if children are not able to talk about their feelings or refer to past events in their lives. The ability to deny is a given unless the family makes a specific effort to alter old family laws and roles. Family members need not have family secrets. When the family has reunited as a result of a recovery process, its members can become even closer, and family life can become even better as long as past and present problems are dealt with in an open and honest manner.

Should family members be involved in a recovery process prior to the addict's sobriety, it is important that they continue in the recovery program even after their chemically dependent person becomes clean and sober. It has taken many years to develop a denial system. While family members may have worked through some of their denial by the time the addict seeks help, it is very natural for them to stop their therapy and revert to old ideas, thinking that once the addict does seek treatment the worst is behind them. Family members, as well as the addicted person, have been perfecting their denial systems for years, and while it may not take as many years to undo that system, the recovery process is an ongoing process.

It is essential for all family members to be familiar with the addict's recovery program. When chemically dependent people regain sobriety, it is most helpful for them to have the support of other recovering people. A recovery program usually involves meetings, whether they are Alcoholics Anonymous meetings, treatment program aftercare meetings, or other supportive groups. Most recovering people need to attend these meetings quite frequently, particularly in the early stages of recovery.

Mike was twelve years old when his father was first getting sober. He had very little denial about his father's alcoholism and was thrilled his father had come to a treatment program. Shortly after his father returned home, Mike reported to his counseling group, "Everything is just really wonderful." He was smiling and had absolutely no problem in the world. I knew his father had been a drinking alcoholic all of Mike's life. Mike believed because Dad was now sober Dad was going to wake up, and no longer being anesthetized, Dad was going to "discover" his twelve-year-old son—a boy he knew very little about. Mike's life just couldn't remain all roses. Mike's mother said that he was having a difficult time in school. One day, I finally confronted Mike, "Mike, things aren't fine, are they?" "Oh yeah, they are just fine," he responded. I said, "No, Mike, things are not just fine. Things are often not good even though a parent gets sober." Finally, Mike said to me (in the form of a picture), "I have a hard time understanding why my dad goes to those meetings every night, and why he is not home." Mike had a lot of expectations, many of which were fantasies, about how he and his father were going to spend so much time together now that his dad was sober. The fact was, in his initial recovery, Mike's dad was so actively involved in Alcoholics Anonymous that he spent less time at home than he had while he was drinking. Mike did not understand; he was confused and very angry, and he immediately reverted to his denial system in order to protect himself from the feelings he was experiencing.

In Mike's case, his father really did need all those meetings. It is not sufficient for a counselor to explain this need to children and spouses. Mike needed his father to share feelings about the meetings and to share his thoughts about sobriety. If parents find they need time away from families to attend meetings, it is important for them to explain and share with the family how vital and necessary this part of their recovery program is for them. In addition, Mike's father still needs to find ways to connect to Mike.

Sharon encountered a similar situation with her children. She found that by telling her kids what she learned at each meeting, making a point to always eat dinner with them, making a point to always say good night, and designating special time every two weeks with each of her two children, she need not reduce the number of meetings she attended, nor feel guilty about her parenting.

Be the reader a parent, sibling, friend, extended family member, or therapist, there are times we cannot change the environment a child is raised in, but we can change what a child believes about him- or herself. Helping a child understand what it is they are reacting to and that they are not the cause of the problems is first and foremost. Helping them understand that their parent has an addiction that is not about choice or about how much they do or do not love their family is important.

We don't want children to generalize what they learn at home, in terms of dysfunctional family rules and roles, to the rest of the world. A ten-year-old may be the adult within the home, but if we can help that ten-year-old be ten outside of the home, we are helping that child to develop more fully.

We need to help children overcome the need to medicate or run from their feelings. We need to assist them in developing problem-solving skills. We need to help them know they are worthy. It sounds like a lot, but if we are willing to offer education about addiction, validate the child in his or her feelings, assist them in problem solving, respond to protection issues, and facilitate a greater support system, we will genuinely create a more resilient child who has a far greater choice about how they will live their life.

Chapter 9

Using Resources

In spite of the knowledge we may gain concerning the impact of addiction in the family and the pain we experience as adult children, there is still the tendency to say "Yes, but . . . yes, but . . . it wasn't that bad. Yes, but . . . no one would really understand. Yes, but . . . I have been out of the home for years now. Yes, but . . . I do really love my parent(s)."

It is true there is always someone with a greater horror story, or who suffered more loss than you. That does not negate *your* pain and loss. There are people who do understand, and it doesn't matter how old you are. You are not betraying your mother, your father, or your family by owning your truth. If there is an act of betrayal, it is with the disease, the addictive disorder. You will betray yourself if you do not allow yourself to heal. You deserve to heal from the pain of the past. You deserve to no longer live a script. You do have choices.

Then come the resistances: "I do want recovery, but I want it to be pain free, thank you." Or, "I want recovery, but I prefer to do it by myself."

Being an adult child, I do genuinely understand. For a moment, imagine the depth of your pain and grief as a strong forceful wind. If you were to stand with ankles and knees held tightly together, back rigidly straight, and arms down by your side in the face of that strong wind, it would easily blow you over. You are probably smart enough to realize that and run for shelter. Most of us run for shelter through work, relationships, drugs or alcohol, sex, or use of money. But if you were to lean forward with feet slightly apart, knees bent, arms slightly away from your body, you may find yourself swaying in the face of that strong wind, but you don't have to run or be blown away. You now have the potential of finding the strength to remain standing.

In addition to balance and flexibility, it is even more likely you will be able to remain standing with the support and help of others. To live in an addictive or otherwise troubled family is to live a life of isolation. You have known isolation for too long. You deserve to allow others to be a part of your process. They will also shine the light and provide the home when recovery is difficult.

Reaching out and making that first contact with a resource is a big step. The act of picking up the phone, dialing the number, and asking to speak to someone who can help you only takes seconds. The process that leads up to making that call for help—the debates with yourself, the mood changes you have experienced, telling yourself you can handle the problems alone, the never-ending, continuous cycle of depression, anger, hope, guilt—all have taken their psychological and physical toll on you and your family. So, for many, it may be months or possibly years before help is sought. But never forget, you are worth that call.

Resources to assist in addressing adult child issues vary. While there have been many books written specifically about adult children of addiction, there are an even greater number that address healing from the pain of troubled families. These books are commonly found in the psychology or self-help sections of major bookstores. There are also Internet sites specific to addiction.

The most readily available services for everyone, regardless of individual circumstances, are the self-help groups. While we do not have the preponderance of adult child or codependency Twelve Step meetings that existed in the 1980s and early 1990s, you may find some in your area. Al-Anon continues to be a viable resource in all of our communities. It is a self-help, Twelve Step–based program for the family and friends of an alcoholic/addict; certainly adult children are welcomed. Should you have a desire to stop drinking or using, or believe you are experiencing a disorder related to food, money, or sex, there are Twelve Step programs specific to those issues as well.

Self-help groups involve no professional counselors and do not document one's involvement. They are free of charge to all who wish to participate. They are groups made up of people who identify with a common problem and are looking for a common solution, a way of helping themselves and each other.

These fellowships have demonstrated themselves to be extremely helpful resources for millions of people. They provide opportunity for children, partners, spouses, or the addicted person to better understand the addiction and how it is affecting their lives. They offer every member a program of recovery, allowing each individual an avenue for feeling better about him- or herself and helping them continue to live more productive lives. Self-help groups offer people an opportunity to realize their experiences and feelings are not unique but, in fact, very similar to problems that each member of the group has experienced.

Each participant is helped through the support and understanding of the group, offered a simple program with guidelines to understand addiction, and given steps to develop and sustain his or her strengths and capabilities. These groups are also used as opportunities for social interaction and feedback from peers.

Another unifying aspect of these groups is that they practice a rule of anonymity. This means who you are is not important, and as a rule, last names are not used. Irrespective of financial worth or social standing, you are considered equal with those fellow beings who suffer the same as you. Thus the groups are able to provide a sensitive nonjudgmental atmosphere where children, spouses, friends, or an addicted person is able to talk about the problems being experienced and can openly express their feelings.

Should you believe you are in a crisis with an addiction, not only will Twelve Step groups be a resource, but you may need to consider a specific program of treatment. Most communities will list addiction information and referral agencies that can assist you. The yellow pages of your telephone directory will be able to offer you local numbers. For a list of Twelve Step groups and other self-help organizations, refer to Resources in the appendix.

I'm glad my dad doesn't drink any more because he talks with me, & I understand him better, I also like the people at A. A. because they don't just walk away from the kids, we go on a lot of picnics with A. A. and they are more fun than being with a bunch of drunk adults!!

In choosing resources, options and needs will vary. Addicted people do get clean and sober, family members do get well, but first, we need to ask for help.

Many people affected by addiction have found the complexity of their life is such that they have strongly benefited from psychotherapy. How do you know if you are one of those who would benefit from therapy rather than just reading on your own or attending a self-help group?

Trust your own perception about whether or not you would benefit from psychotherapy. I would certainly suggest it if you:

- are experiencing signs of depression.
- are engaged in a pattern of self-destructive behaviors that can range from victimization in relationships (repetitive painful relationships) to addictive behaviors.
- have attempted to make constructive changes in your life and have been unable to do so.
- have a history of physical or sexual abuse.

It is imperative to identify a therapist in your community who understands addiction and addictive family systems. If you are unable to identify such a person, contact a local addiction agency to ask for appropriate referrals.

Resources for Children

Children raised with addiction grow up never having shared their closest thoughts or feelings with even their very best friend. It is a very lonely, isolated way of growing up. This loneliness continues into adulthood because no one understood their trauma nor wanted to take the time to talk to these children. People outside of the immediate family have a normal, and perhaps justifiable, fear of meddling in family affairs. Problems between parents and children regarding dress codes, money, or behavior are usually resolved within the confines of the family unit. An "outsider" who takes sides invariably gets the brunt of ill feelings after family members have reconciled these minor differences.

But addiction is not a minor problem.

Addiction is a progressive disease. Untreated, it never gets better, it only gets worse. Becoming an ally to the child is perhaps the first step toward the possibility of recovery for the child and his or her parent(s). Play the role of the listener—listen, console, and help validate the child's feelings. You may not change the home situation, but you can be a vital source in helping children withstand the pressures of the confusion in their family. Offer guidance as it seems appropriate. But remember, the best guidance can be given by a qualified helping professional.

Children are rarely aware of the availability of resources, or they feel immobilized in their powerlessness to act on their own. A child is more likely to follow through with a resource if a trusted person suggests this alternative and if possible helps in locating the specific resources. Anything one does to help bridge the connection will assist the child in getting even more help.

Children come into contact with people who play a variety of roles in their lives—parents, extended family members, friends, neighbors, teachers, counselors, doctors, judges—and each person is in a position to offer different kinds of help and support. The more people make themselves available as knowledgeable, skilled resources, the wider the spectrum and the greater the opportunities for help available to children, whether young, adolescent, or adult.

It is my hope that people not underestimate the amount of difference they can make in the life of a child, no matter how hopeless the situation may appear. A bond with a caregiver is one of the most significant factors as to why some children from addictive families develop strengths and others do not. This is typically someone who allows that child to be age appropriate, to not have to be the adult. This is someone who believes them and will listen. Someone who says in words or behavior, "I care" and "You are important to me." This type of relationship allows that child to internalize worth and, as a consequence, reject the shaming behaviors and messages that may also be coming their way from a troubled family life.

Vanessa, who is now thirty-three, felt strongly about locating a counselor who had worked with her when she was only fifteen. At that time, Vanessa's parents were living on the streets and she had been put into a group home for approximately three months. She wanted to say thank-you. When the counselor asked what she remembered specifically about the counseling, she replied, "I have no idea what you did, but I know that you loved me."

Sometimes it is not what we do; it is what we feel and then have the ability to convey. Genuinely believing she was loved was the intangible gift that this young woman would hang on to and from which she would find strength. That was more than she had ever experienced. And then she pulled out a journal and said, "You did ask me to keep a journal and to this day I do that." The journaling would be a daily source of release and possibly strength but having felt loved was most important.

It is my contention children growing up with addiction suffer unhealthy consequences due to lack of involvement with other people, not from concerned involvement.

National Association for Children of Alcoholics

Since the original writing of *It Will Never Happen to Me,* a major nonprofit association has been created to advocate on behalf of children affected by alcohol and drug dependency. Since 1983, the National Association for Children of Alcoholics (NACOA) has been providing information and education to help COAs of all ages. NACOA is a policy development center and a central point of input for children's health and welfare advocates and service providers who address populations of COAs. Over the years it has provided significant materials to school systems, interfaith communities, and medical schools and practitioners. A wonderful way to advocate for children of addicted parents would be to become a member of this organization. (Refer to Resources in the appendix.)

School Systems

Schools have the greatest access to the largest number of children. For that reason alone, they are extremely viable resources for identifying children affected by addiction in the family. If you are a concerned teacher, counselor, or administrator, you are in a position to influence children individually through direct contact or in large numbers through the school system. Teachers can recognize children who have problems at home by an assessment of their behavior and appearance—children who have problems with their schoolwork, who come to school sleepy or emotionally distraught, or who are improperly clothed or groomed. They may be the children who are "too good to be true" and/or those who speak about the subject directly or indirectly. Teachers often overhear what children say to each other on the playground or in the hallways. Impressions are formed and pieces of the puzzle fit together. Often, it seems apparent that little can be done to change the home environment, but we can provide relief for the child in need by being willing to listen, offering them understanding, or by simply giving solace. Giving a child validation, honesty, and sincerity is offering them hope.

School counselors are in a better position than teachers to discuss issues about the home directly. Principals are in a position to see that staff members are appropriately trained to be more effective resources. All staff and faculty are in a position to ask the administration for assistance in utilizing outside resources to assist in identifying these children and appropriate referral networks that focus on addictive disorders. Along with many of the curriculums, support systems are developed with outside agencies to aid in the training and implementation of such programs. Many schools have student assistance programs specifically designed to work with children impacted by substance abuse and seen as high-risk for addiction. To learn more about student assistance programs, refer to Resources in the appendix.

Taking Responsibility

Children affected by addiction will be adequately addressed and helped only when we, lay people and professionals alike, begin to take responsibility. Everyone who has access to these children needs to take some responsibility. The possibilities are many and greatly vary, but all give validation to a child.

- Allow the child to be age appropriate
- Validate the child's feelings
- Listen when the child wants to talk
- Acknowledge the child's reality
- Talk with a family member
- Ask the board you sit on to address the issue
- Ask a clergyperson to address this issue with peers
- Ask a physician to identify the impact addiction has on a family when it is recognized
- Discuss addiction when identified
- Suggest and refer to Twelve Step programs or treatment when indicated
- Develop specific treatment for children of addiction

These actions take a willingness to become involved and a willingness to help improve the quality of someone else's life.

It is of paramount importance that resources for children do not underestimate the impact they have on a child, no matter how limited in power or time they perceive themselves to be. Few helping professionals ever have all of the ideal means, staff, space, money, or time necessary to develop the comprehensive services desired. But if each assesses what can be done with the means at hand, they can actualize resources on the spot. With even a little greater effort, intermediate and long-range goals can be developed. To say "We just can't do it all" is delinquent behavior on our part, which is really saying "We don't care enough."

Everyone who has access to a child needs to take responsibility. Resources need to be supportive of each other. If you are willing to ask yourself what help you can provide within the structure of your life and your work, then you are taking the first step.

Together we can break the Don't Talk rule and break the generational cycle of addiction.

I FEEL LIKE I'VE BEEN ON A ROLLACOASTER FOR A REAL LONG TIME. I WANT OFF.

JANICE, 44

Appendices

Problem Solving Form

Resources

Suggested Reading

Problem Solving Form

Situations	Possibilities
WHAT IF . . .	1.
	2.
	3.
WHAT IF . . .	1.
	2.
	3.
WHAT IF . . .	1.
	2.
	3.

Resources

There are currently several million recovering people around the planet attending Twelve Step or other recovery meetings on a regular basis. It is relatively easy to find a meeting in any city or country if you know where to look. The World Wide Web provides a variety of recovery resources. The following is a directory of recovery and self-help organizations.

Adult Children of Alcoholics
310.534.1815 • www.adultchildren.org

Al-Anon / Alateen
888.4ALANON • www.al-anon.org

Alcoholics Anonymous
212.870.3400 • www.alcoholics-anonymous.org

Co-Anon Family Groups
www.co-anon.org

Co-dependents Anonymous
www.codependents.org

Co-Sex Addicts Anonymous (COSA)
www.cosa-recovery.org

Cocaine Anonymous
800.347.7991 • www.ca.org

Debtors Anonymous
781.453.2743 • www.debtorsanonymous.org

Eating Addictions Anonymous
202.882.6528 • www.dcregistry.com/users/eatingaddictions

Emotions Anonymous
651.647.9712 • www.emotionsanonymous.org

Families Anonymous
800.736.9805 • www.familiesanonymous.org

Gamblers Anonymous
213.386.8789 • www.gamblersanonymous.org

Marijuana Anonymous
800.766.6779 • www.marijuana-anonymous.org

Narcotics Anonymous
818.773.9999 • www.na.org

National Association for Children of Alcoholics
888.554.2627 • www.nacoa.org

National Council for Couple & Family Recovery
NCFFR@hotmail.com

National Council on Alcoholism & Drug Dependence
800.NCA-Call • www.ncadd.org

National Council on Sex Addiction & Compulsivity
770.541.9912 • www.ncsac.org

National Student Assistance Programs
800.453.7733

Nicotine Anonymous
866.536.4539 • www.nicotine-anonymous.org

Overeaters Anonymous
505.891.2664 • www.overeatersanonymous.org

Pills Anonymous
212.874.0700 • pillsanonymous.com

Rational Recovery System
800.303.2873 • www.rational.org/recovery

Recovering Couples Anonymous
510.336.3300 • www.recovering-couples.org

Recovery Online
www.onlinerecovery.org

Runaway & Suicide Hotline
800.621.4000

Sage Times Addictions, Mental Health, Medications
www.sagetimes.com

Sex & Love Addicts Anonymous (SLAA)
781.255.8825 • www.slaafws.org

Sex Addicts Anonymous
800.477.8191 • www.sexaa.org

Sex Anonymous Family Groups (S-Anon)
615.773.0909 • www.sanon.org

Sexaholics Anonymous (SA)
615.331.6230 • www.sa.org

Sexual Addiction Resources
www.sexhelp.com

Sexual Compulsives Anonymous (SCA)
800.977.HEAL • www.sca-recovery.org

Survivors of Incest Anonymous
410.893.3322 • www.siawso.org

Women for Sobriety
215.536.8026 • www.womenforsobriety.org

Suggested Reading

Children of Addiction

Adult Children: The Secrets of Dysfunctional Families, John and Linda Friel, Health Communications, 1988.

Children of Alcoholics: Selected Readings, Volume II, Robert J. Ackerman et al., NACOA, 2000.

Perfect Daughters: Adult Daughters of Alcoholics, Robert J. Ackerman, Health Communications, 1989.

Safe Passage: Recovery for Adult Children of Alcoholics, Stephanie Brown, John Wiley & Sons, 1992.

Silent Sons: A Book for and about Men, Robert J. Ackerman, Fireside, 1994.

The Resilient Self: How Survivors of Troubled Families Rise above Adversity, Steven J. and Sybil Wolin, Villard Books, 1993.

Codependence

Another Chance: Hope and Health for the Alcoholic Family, 2d. ed., Sharon Wegscheider-Cruse, Science and Behavior, 1989.

Boundaries: Where You End and I Begin, Anne Katherine, Fine Communications, 1998.

Bradshaw on the Family: A Revolutionary Way of Self-Discovery, John E. Bradshaw, Health Communications, 1988.

Codependent No More: How to Stop Controlling Others and Start Caring for Yourself, Melody Beattie, Hazelden, 1992.

Facing Codependence: What It Is, Where It Comes from, How It Sabotages Our Lives, Pia Mellody et al., Harper San Francisco, 1989.

Facing Love Addiction: Giving Yourself the Power to Change the Way You Love, Pia Mellody et al., Harper San Francisco, 1992.

Healing the Child Within: Discovery and Recovery for Adult Children of Dysfunctional Families, Charles L. Whitfield, M.D., Health Communications, 1989.

Is It Love or Is It Addiction? 2d ed., Brenda Schaeffer, Hazelden, 1997.

The Betrayal Bond: Breaking Free of Exploitive Relationships, Patrick Carnes, Health Communications, 1997.

The Drama of the Gifted Child: The Search for the True Self, rev. and updtd., Alice Miller, Basic Books, 1996.

Parenting

Kids' Power, Too: Words to Grow By, Jerry Moe et al., Imagin Works, 1996.

Parents, Teens and Boundaries: How to Draw the Line, Jane Bluestein, Health Communications, 1993.

Self-Esteem: A Family Affair, Jean Illsley Clarke, Hazelden, 1998.

The Parent's Little Book of Lists: Do's and Don'ts of Effective Parenting, Jane Bluestein, Health Communications, 1997.

Addiction

Contrary to Love: Helping the Sexual Addict, Patrick Carnes, Hazelden, 1989.

Deadly Odds: Recovery from Compulsive Gambling, Ken Estes and Michael Brubaker, Fireside Parkside, 1998.

Don't Call It Love: Recovery from Sexual Addiction, Patrick Carnes, Bantam, 1992.

Educating Yourself about Alcohol and Drugs: A People's Primer, rev. ed., Marc Schuckit, Perseus, 1998.

Lonely All the Time: Recognizing, Understanding, and Overcoming Sex Addiction, for Addicts and Co-Dependents, Ralph H. Earle and Gregory Crowe, Pocket Books, 1998.

Out of the Shadows: Understanding Sexual Addiction, 3rd ed., Patrick Carnes, Hazelden, 2001.

Stage II Recovery: Life Beyond Addiction, Earnie Larsen, Harper & Row San Francisco, 1985.

Women, Sex, and Addiction: A Search for Love, Charlotte Davis Kasl, Harper & Row, 1989.

Recovery

Compelled to Control: Recovering Intimacy in Broken Relationships, rev. ed., J. Keith Miller, Health Communications, 1997.

Craving for Ecstasy: The Consciousness and Chemistry of Escape, Harvey B. Milkman and Stanley Sunderwirth, Jossey Bass, Inc., 1998.

Emotional Incest Syndrome: What to Do When a Parent's Love Rules Your Life, Patricia Love, Bantam Doubleday Dell, 1991.

Emotional Intelligence, Daniel Goleman, Bantam, 1995.

Facing Shame: Families in Recovery, Merle A. Fossum and Marilyn J. Mason, Norton, 1989.

Healing the Shame That Binds You, John Bradshaw, Health Communications, 1988.

I Don't Want to Talk about It: Overcoming the Secret Legacy of Male Depression, Terrence Real, Fireside, 1998.

Mind over Mood: Change How You Feel by Changing the Way You Think, Dennis Greenberger and Christine A. Padesky, Guilford Press, 1995.

Moodswing: Dr. Fieve on Depression, rev. ed., Ronald R. Fieve, M.D., Bantam, 1997.

The Courage to Heal: A Guide for Women Survivors of Child Sexual Abuse, 3rd, rev. and updtd., Ellen Bass and Laura Davis, Harperperennial, 1994.

The Feeling Good Handbook, rev. ed., David D. Burns, M.D., Plume, 1999.

The Grief Recovery Handbook, John W. James and Frank Cherry, Harperperennial, 1998.

The Verbally Abusive Relationship: How to Recognize It and How to Respond, 2d exp. ed., Patricia Evans, Adams Media Corp., 1996.

Also by Claudia Black, Ph.D.

Books

A Hole in the Sidewalk
Anger Guide
Changing Course
It's Never Too Late to Have a Happy Childhood
My Dad Loves Me, My Dad Has a Disease
Repeat After Me
Relapse Toolkit

CDs

A Time for Healing from Abandonment and Shame
Imageries
Letting Go Imageries
Putting the Past Behind

Videos

Anger
Addiction in the Family
The Baggage Cart
Breaking the Silence
Children of Denial
Healing from Childhood Sexual Abuse
The History of Addiction
The Legacy of Addiction
Process of Recovery
Relapse: The Illusion of Immunity
Relationship Series
Roles
Shame

Books, videos, and audios are available through:
MAC Publishing
PMB 346, 321 High School Road N.E.
Bainbridge Island, WA 98110
800.698.0148 Toll-free
206.842.6303 Voice
206.842.6235 Fax
Online Catalog: www.claudiablack.com

To arrange a speaking engagement with Dr. Black, contact Claudja, Inc.
800.698.0148 Toll-free
206.842.6303 Voice
206.842.6235 Fax
cblack@nwlink.com

About the Author

Claudia Black, Ph.D., is a renowned lecturer, author, and trainer, internationally recognized for her pioneering and contemporary work with family systems and addictive disorders. Her work encompasses the interest of both the professional and lay audience. She has written nine books and produced a multitude of educational videos in which she speaks to the issue of addictive disorders. She currently presents workshops and seminars and consults to addiction treatment programs in the United States and abroad.

Dr. Black has received numerous awards for her work, ranging from the annual SECAD Award, the National Council on Alcohol and Drug Dependency Communicator of the Year, and the Marty Mann Award. She serves on numerous advisory boards and is the past chairperson for the National Association for Children of Alcoholics.

She resides on a lovely island in the Pacific Northwest with her husband, Jack, their cats Ashley and Bleau, and their dogs Quinn and Katie.

Hazelden Publishing and Educational Services is a division of the Hazelden Foundation, a not-for-profit organization. Since 1949, Hazelden has been a leader in promoting the dignity and treatment of people afflicted with the disease of chemical dependency.

The mission of the foundation is to improve the quality of life for individuals, families, and communities by providing a national continuum of information, education, and recovery services that are widely accessible; to advance the field through research and training; and to improve our quality and effectiveness through continuous improvement and innovation.

Stemming from that, the mission of this division is to provide quality information and support to people wherever they may be in their personal journey—from education and early intervention, through treatment and recovery, to personal and spiritual growth.

Although our treatment programs do not necessarily use everything Hazelden publishes, our bibliotherapeutic materials support our mission and the Twelve Step philosophy upon which it is based. We encourage your comments and feedback.

The headquarters of the Hazelden Foundation are in Center City, Minnesota. Additional treatment facilities are located in Chicago, Illinois; New York, New York; Plymouth, Minnesota; St. Paul, Minnesota; and West Palm Beach, Florida. At these sites, we provide a continuum of care for men and women of all ages. Our Plymouth facility is designed specifically for youth and families.

For more information on Hazelden, please call **1-800-257-7800.** Or you may access our World Wide Web site on the Internet at **www.hazelden.org.**